ED CUSHMAN

LOSING A HAND

iUniverse books may be ordered through booksellers or by contacting:

iUniverse
1663 Liberty Drive
Bloomington, IN 47403
www.iuniverse.com
844-349-9409

ISBN: 978-1-6632-3005-8 (sc)
ISBN: 978-1-6632-3006-5 (e)

Library of Congress Control Number: 2021920448

Print information available on the last page.

iUniverse rev. date: 10/04/2021

INTRODUCTION

You are about to read a true story. It's about myself and other upper extremity amputees. My intentional hand amputation occurred in 1973. This was long before the condition known as Amputee Identity Disorder (AID) or Body Integrity Identity Disorder (BIID) was identified. Now that more is known about these conditions, those who have them are fortunately no longer thrown into a psychotic category.

The BME Encyclopedia defines Body Integrity Identity Disorder, or BIID, as a psychological condition in which an individual actively pursues an elective amputation. Individuals with this condition experience the persistent desire to have their body physically match the idealized image they have of themselves.

These conditions are characterized by an intense desire to be an amputee. These people often feel incomplete even though they have all of their limbs. Sufferers of AID and BIID are sometimes driven to seek accidents, self-injury or surgery to remove the unwanted limb(s). They have an idealized picture of themselves as missing a limb, and often feel that they are somehow 'incomplete' or 'imperfect', so long as their healthy limb remains.

These individuals often relate that their feelings and urges have persisted since childhood. They can often recall seeing an amputee as early as 4 or 5 years of age. This sighting remains with them throughout their life. It's thought that this may be the trigger for their feelings.

These individuals are afraid to tell anyone about these feelings for fear of ridicule and rejection. They often pretend to be an amputee by binding up a limb to simulate the amputation. They may have the feeling that they are alone in the world with their desire to be an amputee. Few ever "come out" to their friends or loved ones. Most of the above also applies to me.

When I originally wrote this story, I set out to tell of my "accident" and how it affected me and how upper-extremity injuries have affected others. By the time it was actually about to become printed in book form in 2002, I no longer felt the need to hide my "deed" which happened some 30 years before. I had proven to the world (if that was necessary) that my amputation had no adverse affect on my abilities or my success in life. My only hesitation in revealing myself was the possible hurt I might have caused those close to me who had thought this was a true accident. Since this was so long ago, most had either passed away (my parents) or were out of touch with me over time. So after much deliberation, I decided that the true story about what I did might be of some help to others who also felt the same as I about wanting to be an amputee and that at last I would reveal my story by publishing my manuscript.

Now that this desire is becoming recognized as a true psychological disorder I think it is time for the world to become more accepting of those afflicted so they can feel more comfortable in coming forward and move to help them through treatment or amputation. They need counseling so they can either resolve their conflicts or have the body part removed so they can get on with their lives. There are many moral issues involved here, which is beyond the scope of this book.

When I received copies of this first printing I gave books to carefully selected friends and neighbors without revealing my story beforehand. Most of them took my 'coming out' in stride, though they were a bit taken back as I had proven to be a sane and faithful friend. Their thoughts usually ran along the lines..."but sane people don't do this sort of thing..." Still a few couldn't accept the fact that I did the amputation on purpose. In time however, they have come to accept me and my condition and we are once again friends, though their rejection hurt me. At the same time I feel that a few of my friends will never be able handle my true story so I have chosen not to intentionally cause them pain by telling them. If they somehow do come across my book, so be it. Hopefully time will heal for them also. Not everyone is ready for voluntary amputation, no matter what the reasons.

Since my 'coming out' I have made numerous new friends on the internet in this underground world of sufferers. It is indeed true that, as I've come to realize, I'm not the only one who feels this way. I am however, amazed at how "we" are spread throughout the far corners of the world and speak many languages. These are also some of the most intelligent and sincere people I have ever come to know. They too felt the need to be an amputee and have carried it out against all norms of acceptance.

My story begins when I meet a teen neighbor who had recently lost his hand because of a pipe bomb accident. In the course of getting to know him and the problems he had dealing with his loss, my BIID was rekindled and prompted me to saw off my hand intentionally. The ensuing text covers my experience and well as other accidental amputees. This was long before anything was known about this disorder. My story was written from this perspective. The final chapter discusses AID and BIID and contains experiences from several who carried out their own amputations. You will hear what drove them and how this disorder affected their lives before and after their "deed."

CHAPTER 1

Learning From Pete

As a child of perhaps 5 years, I can remember standing at the check-out counter at a supermarket with my mother. The bag boy had only one hand. This was my first encounter with an amputee, and I will remember it for ever. Many other BIID sufferers have expressed similar experiences as children. This seems to be a common denominator.

The second encounter with a "one-hander" that made an impression on me was when I met fifteen-year-old Pete the evening he came over with his younger brother Tom. They came over to socialize. I had known Tom on an occasional basis for several months. There were seven children in the family. The parents had divorced and the father was living out in the country. The kids would go out to visit "dad" as often as they could.

Young Tom never mentioned his older brother Pete before. As they came in the front door, I could see that Pete's right arm was in a cast below his elbow and his hand was missing. As we talked, he said he lost his hand in Vietnam. He was tall, and looked old enough to have been in the service. He was thin and had a shy, reserved manor. I had worked down in the Pacific for several years, so I attempted to make conversation about places that I had assumed he had also seen. He was reluctant to talk about them, so I dropped the subject. I had the feeling that he felt uncomfortable talking about this, so I didn't press the issue because we didn't know each other very well.

Some time later, I learned through neighborhood teen friends that he didn't lose his hand in Vietnam, but on his dad's farm, about twenty-five miles from the town in which we lived. Pete was making a pipe bomb, with gun powder, when it exploded, shredding his right hand and several fingers on his left. Though he looked big enough to have been in Nam, he was in fact just 15.

After Pete recovered from his injuries, and his arm healed, he returned to spend the summer on his dad's farm. He often went into town to his mother's home for visits with his brothers and sisters. They all enjoyed trips out to the farm, often staying for several weeks when school was out in the summer.

I soon learned that Pete, the oldest of the boys, avoided public encounters if at all possible. He felt uncomfortable with people he didn't know. He seemed to feel his performance with one hand was always being scrutinized by those around him. He felt that if he should fail at some task, he might be ridiculed. His feelings of self-worth and esteem were really weak. The loss of his right hand only reinforced these feelings. This may have been the result of the conflict between his parents that eventually ended with their divorce. The seclusion of his dad's farm was the perfect place to avoid social contact and the numerous and often frustrating situations he often encountered in town.

Pete's mom was a nurse. She made him casts to wear over the end of his arm. It wasn't that he needed them for medical reasons, his arm had healed well. The bomb he was making shredded his right hand, so the surgeon tried to save as much of the end of his arm as possible. It ended just below the wrist bone. The casts he wore on his arm seemed to serve as an "emotional bandage" for Pete, providing an excuse to avoid dealing with his condition. The cast was also an effective way to hide his injury from the world. He seemed to feel that an arm in a cast was more acceptable than one without a hand on the end of it. Also, a cast would hide the incision and red marks where the stitches were, thus avoiding any comments about them. I hadn't seen him wear any type of artificial arm or prosthesis during his numerous visits to my place.

Soon Pete felt comfortable enough to visit by himself with out his younger brother Tom. While in town, Pete didn't have much to do. Shopping in stores was an uncomfortable experience, rather than a fun time. Children would, at times, stop and openly stare at his arm. This was a perfectly normal reaction for their age. An innocent question such as, "What happened to your arm?," was very embarrassing for Pete. He wanted to get away as fast as possible. Encounters such as these, reinforced his feelings of guilt, bringing his attention back to an event in his life that he badly wanted to forget.

I encouraged Pete to stop in as often as he liked. Seeing him brought back my childhood memories of the shopping trip to a grocery store when I was about five or six years old and the bag boy who was missing a hand. This made a big impression on me, as it was the first time I had ever seen anyone with only one hand. Ever after, I developed a secret admiration for such people. Now I had one of these very special people actually visiting me in my own home!

Pete was a big, but gentle person. He loved the outdoors, hunting and animals. We were very much alike in this respect. I think this was why we became good friends. I had never married and he was just a teen so we soon developed a close, but guarded bond. He had several head of beef cattle out on his dads' farm. It was a great place for us to visit whenever we had any spare time. Through these fun times in the country, a friendship evolved that allowed me to develop a close understanding of him and to eventually learn why he felt so uncomfortable in social situations with people that he didn't know.

In his work, however, Pete was quite confident and always eager to get the job done. He wasn't reluctant to attempt new projects around the farm. He did have confidence about his own abilities. Perhaps too much at times. It may have been his overconfidence that got him into trouble with the gunpowder.

Over the months, our mutual trust grew. We often had casual discussions about what the future might bring. One such occasion was on a warm summer night. We were driving on a quiet back road in my van after dinner, not going any place in particular. Our conversation eventually got around to the type of work he might do some day. In an off-handed way, he talked about what troubled him most, deep down inside;

"What do you think about using a hook if you have only one hand?" he asked meekly.

My heart jumped! This was the first time that he ever mentioned a prosthesis. I had hoped he would eventually talk about it. I didn't want to push him, by asking about this. I felt he would talk when he was ready, when he had my confidence.

"It seems that it could be a big help, especially with things like using a shovel or a wheel porrow, I said, containing my enthusiasm. I felt bad that he didn't feel psychologically comfortable using a hook, and often wondered if he ever would. I could sense that he was testing me, to find out how I felt about it.

"Look how much easier it would be to drive a tractor," I said. "You could hang onto the steering wheel and lower the plow at the same time," I was trying to be as positive as I could, without being obvious. In reality, he might have been using a prosthesis on the farm, when his friends from town weren't around. I didn't know.

"Yeah, I guess so," was his response, as if he wasn't all that convinced.

He re-lit his corncob pipe as we drove slowly through one of our favorite hunting areas. It seemed easier to talk about inner feelings in the darkness of the night. The good smells of the pipe tobacco that we both liked eased the situation. I suspected he might have an artificial arm, but because he never wanted to talk about it, I too felt uncomfortable, and didn't want to offend him. We both were very sensitive of each others' feelings. Because I valued his friendship, and was anxious for him to overcome his awkwardness about his arm, I let him lead the way, even though it was frustrating for me to see him fumble with the use of one hand. I supposed that he was really handicapped by his loss, especially since he still had his arm in a cast below his elbow. Because he was uncomfortable talking about it himself, I assumed the worst about his abilities. At this point in his life, he still needed the sympathy his cast would gain him among those whom he didn't know intimately.

Gaining confidence after a few puffs, he continued, "I've got this prosthesis. It's kind of ugly, but it makes it easier for me to do things."

His tone of voice had a detached and off-handed quality. It was as if someone else, rather than Pete was doing the talking.

I was familiar with the term, "prothesis". A Greek word meaning, "body replacement part."

"Hmm," I said eagerly, prodding him on, "but what difference does it make what it looks like, if it works for you?"

A negative response from me at this point would have been very crushing to his ego. It would have confirmed his inner feelings of guilt and low self-worth.

"I use it when I'm on the farm. That way I can get accustomed to it," he added.

It seems that Pete had been fitted with a prostheses for some time, but never wore it in public. He was becoming more accepting of himself and his condition now. He was gaining more confidence. It was about 6 months since his accident.

I was quite excited when he came over to my house one evening, after dinner. He was wearing his prosthesis.

"Wow, what's that you got there?" I said excitedly.

This was the first time I had ever seen one close up. I wanted to learn all about it, but he was reluctant to openly discuss it.

It's my prosthesis, the hook is made of stainless steel."

At least he was wearing it. I had to restrain my curiosity and let Pete reveal it at his own pace. It was a delicate situation.

"It looks really neat!" I said, trying to react very positive about it.

I could see by the reaction on his face that he was glad I liked it. A negative response from me at this point would have been devastating for Pete. His voice suddenly became more animated.

"Yea, It's a lot easier to steer that old tractor of dad's with my hook. It turns like a tank with out power steering."

Never having any children of my own, I had grown close to Pete. We became sort of "special buddies." He grew to trust me as I was careful never to make fun of him or put him down, especially about his missing hand. I really enjoyed our times together, as they were fulfilling the secret admiration I've always felt for amputees.

The next Friday, after work, I picked Pete up at his mom's, and we drove out to the farm for the weekend. The ride gave us time to talk in confidence once again. I was pleased to see that he was still wearing his arm. I could sense his eagerness to try new things with his hook, to show it off. I got the feeling that this was going to be a very interesting two days. Now he could be equal to everyone else in his abilities, (at least it seemed to me). We lit up our pipes as we drove through the rolling farm land. The trees were showing their best fall colors. Our spirits were never higher.

"Next week hunting starts you know," he said eagerly. "Have you got your licence?

"No, but I had better get on it! Can you work a gun alright with your arm? I asked encouragingly.

"Sure, I just rest it here on top of my hook where the rubber bands are. They sort of keeps it from sliding around. I've seen lots of deer in the woods behind dad's place," he said with lots of zest.

His enthusiasm made me feel good. It seemed that at last he was looking forward to something in his life after his accident.

Pete had evidently been using his hook for some time. He didn't seem to be having any difficulty handling his pipe. He held the bowl with his hook while he lit it with a match held in his left hand. He was missing the end of his thumb and 2 fingers, but there was enough left to do the job. It was kind of neat that he could now do things for himself that otherwise were previously difficult. He did well before, using one hand to light his pipe, but I could sense his feelings of pride and accomplishment at his new found ability. He could pack the tobacco with the end of his hook while it was lit, and not even burn his finger! I complimented him on this feat as something special that only he could do. Now he had the advantage for a change.

When it was time to feed the animals in the barn, Pete was eager to display his new abilities and strength. He tossed the bales of hay down from the loft with ease. He actually was able to carry them more easily than I. The steel hook was tremendously strong. He didn't have to worry about the tough bailing twine cutting his hand. He forked silage with new-found energy. His type of terminal device was called a "farmers'" hook. It sure was well designed. It had a round portion that he could use to grasp a fork handle. We both had more fun doing the chores than ever before.

The muscles in his right arm had grown very weak from not being used for such a long time. Now that he was using them again, they would begin to recover and grow stronger every day.

After chores, he could now wash up by himself. Before, without his prosthesis, his dad had to wash his hand for him. It sure got greasy working on machinery. Maybe even twice as dirty, since it was doing the work of two hands! Now he could use a sponge, holding it with his hook to scrub his own hand.

Tending the wood stove was easy. The stainless steel hook could touch hot things without being damaged.

"I'll bet you can't do this!" he said, opening the hot door of the stove with his hook.

Taking hot pans out of the oven was fun too. He would need only a pot holder, or none at all! He was becoming more confident and self-sufficient. Pete even began to feel somewhat special for a change. He was doing things that the rest of the family couldn't do. He was able to do them because of the prosthesis that he dreaded for so long.

Fall was my favorite time of the year. The patches of woods that dot the countryside become ablaze with color. Grouse hunting was one of the best excuses, (if one was needed) to get outdoors. Pete and his younger brother Tom, were avid hunters. We had many choice hunting spots near the farm.

One Saturday morning as we gathered around the living room stove to dress to go out, Pete had his youngest brother Tim tie his boots as usual. I was a bit surprised at this, as Pete was quite able to most everything for himself, now that he was using his hook every day. I tend to become impatient at times, expecting activities such as learning to do things with a hook instead of a hand, to become an instant reality. Though Pete's progress was moving along rapidly now, I often felt he should have been more competent.

The next morning I had an idea while putting on my boots. I watched Pete for a minuet, then said, "Pete, why don't you try this?"

I used a pair of pliers in my right hand as he would have used his hook. I gripped the laces with the pliers and tied my boots. Even though I never thought of, or tried this technique before, I found that it worked just fine. It would have been the logical thing for me to do if I had a hook, instead of a hand.

It wasn't long before Pete was tying his own boots faster than anyone else. It was a matter of having the self-confidence needed to attempt these new things. Sure, there were some risks involved - risks that were often embarrassing for Pete if he failed in front of others. Then, there is the old saying, "nothing ventured, nothing gained..." This is especially true when one has to learn new ways of doing everyday tasks.

Relating my ideas about how to do things with one hand and one hook was a delicate process for me. If over done, or not presented in an acceptable manner to Pete, he might have interpreted them as being demeaning. He needed all the confidence I could give him.

Thoughts such as, "I never think of these things myself, I guess I'm pretty dumb..." could have turned the situation into a negative learning process, and actually impede his progress. It could have even ruined our close friendship.

In order to avoid this, I would make suggestions such as, "Maybe you could try..." or, "you know what might work..." I was careful never to say anything negative about what he was doing. He was very sensitive in this respect, and would immediately become defensive. Because I realized this, I used the utmost care to always encourage him and offer compliments whenever possible. At the same time, I often felt much the same way he did about things, and had a great deal of empathy for him and his new awkward physical condition. At the same time I was beginning to realize that missing a hand wasn't all that bad. Although I had always admired amputees, I was now being forced to confront the every day tasks of one-handers on a very personal level. I was getting to even like the challenges this new world offered!

One Sunday evening, after returning from a weekend out at the farm, I dropped Pete off at his mom's house and continued home, a few blocks away. I puttered around the house for a while, then began to wonder what to do for dinner, after a cue from my stomach.

The phone rang and I picked it up, "Hello?" I said in an extra pleasant tone of voice that I often used when I felt it was a friend, but didn't know who it might be.

"Hi, this is Pete," was the response in a voice that I hadn't heard for at least 20 minuets, "Watcha doing?"

"Oh, kind of wandering around the house, thinking about what to do for dinner."

"Ya, (his family background was German also) me too. No one is home," he said in his usual gentle tone of voice.

"Why don't you come over and we can get something together to eat," I suggested.

"I didn't think you'd want to eat with me tonight, after being with me all weekend," he said with a hint of guilt in his voice.

I could sense that he felt grateful for the close friendship we had, he didn't have many other close friends.

"I had a great time, Pete," I said eagerly, "You're one of the good guys. I'd be honored to have you over."

I could sense the warm glow in him as he accepted the offer and said he'd be over in a few minutes. Nothing in the world is more comforting than the understanding of a close friend.

Pete and I both enjoyed hunting. I'm not sure if we liked the hunting process itself, or just being out-of-doors. One Saturday afternoon, I was walking on a grassy path at the edge of a field, and Pete was walking through the woods about four meters from me. I couldn't see him, as the trees and brush were quite thick.

Grouse hunting requires that one be quick and accurate with a gun. the bird often waits till the last moment, as it is approached, before it roars up and away from you. There is little time to think and consider a plan of action. It is best to keep your gun cradled in your arm, finger on the safety, ready to shoot in an instant.

Pete had the necessary quick reflexes and was an avid hunter. The fact that he could not grasp the receiver of his shotgun, because he had a hook instead of a hand, made little difference in his shooting ability. He rested the gun on his forearm, and was a very accurate shot.

Suddenly I heard the drum of wings, followed by a quick shot, then a cry. My first thought was that Pete had somehow shot himself. My heart jumped and began to beat faster. As I made my way though the trees, I saw him lying on the ground.

"Are you alright?" I asked uncertainly. I noticed blood oozing from his nose, down onto his face.

"I guess so," he said rather sheepishly. "I must have shot before I had the gun tight against my shoulder and the recoil banged my nose or something. It all happened so fast..."

Well, we never did find that bird. I'll always remember our hunting experiences and how my friend with the hook could shoot better than I with two good hands!

With the new-found confidence Pete developed over the summer, he moved back home to the city and even returned to school that fall. I could tell by the smiles on his face that he was once again becoming his own person. He no longer had to hide behind a plaster cast on the end of his arm. He had a bright stainless steel hook that was indestructible, and he now used it!

The first summer after Pete began wearing his arm, he was reluctant to wear a short-sleeved shirt, exposing his prosthesis. Just as acceptance of the loss of a hand come in stages, Petes' self-confidence returned in stages. He always wore a long-sleeved shirt, even in the heat of summer. Eventually he became confident enough to graduate to short-sleeved shirts. It took several years for him to gain enough confidence to sit around home without wearing his prosthesis, allowing the stump of his arm to be seen by all.

Pete was now old enough to drive a car, and was eager to start practicing for his drivers test. I had a manual transmission in my car and offered the use of the vehicle for his practice driving sessions. If he was to have an unrestricted license, he had to take his test in a car with a standard or manual transmission. His mom's car was an automatic. He had been driving for several years around the farm and surrounding countryside, and was familiar with the mechanics of it all. The formality of city streets and traffic laws were new, however.

Pete had little difficulty shifting with his hook. It was a matter of pushing the floor-mounted lever forward, or pulling it back. It wasn't necessary for him to grasp the ball at the top of the shift lever as is done with a hand. The necessary lever movement could be accomplished without using the knob.

After several weeks of practice, I felt Pete was ready for the exam. Suspense filled the air on the day of the test. I left work early and picked Pete up at his home and drove him over to the city hall building. We walked up to the second floor where the motor vehicle department held exams once a week.

I waited expectantly while Pete was out on the road test with the examiner. This driving test was just one of the many hurtles Pete faced as he work his way back into society - a society that often assumes you are unable until you prove you are competent.

In Pete's case, he was young, active and healthy. He was physically able to do anything he wanted to do. Mentally, he was having difficulty performing in public and wasn't feeling comfortable with the way he looked without a right hand. This wasn't a condition that was unique to him alone. Most amputees experience these difficulties to some degree.

As Pete and the examiner entered the room, Pete's eyes avoided mine... a bad sign. I felt so sure that he was shifting as well as any two-handed person. What was the big deal about shifting a car with a hook? I was beginning to feel prejudice toward the examiner. If he only knew how well Pete could handle a tractor on a bumpy corn field, and even plow by moonlight... my blood was beginning to boil.

Not a word was exchanged as we walked down the steps to the car. Once inside with the doors closed, he began to talk, much to my relief, "I didn't have any trouble shifting, he even said I did it real well."

"Wow, I'm glad to hear that. I was ready to wring his neck," I said with much relief. "Well, what went wrong then?"

"I turned onto a one-way street from the wrong lane," he said almost apologetically. "I have to come back again in two weeks for another test."

"Is that all? That is almost great! I mean, I was so worried that you would have some sort of trouble shifting the car. Anybody can make a wrong turn and fail the test!"

So it was back to driving around town, like "two little old ladies", as we used to joke. We concentrated on the tricky one-way streets this time. His shifting was now taken for granted. His confidence grew. he knew what to expect on the test. His focus shifted away from his steel farmers' hook to the street where it belonged. A driving test can be pretty tense for any teen with two good hands, but I felt this one-hander would make it this time.

We felt pretty good that afternoon when we got home from his second test. He passed with flying colors. The examiner complimented him on his excellent ability at the wheel. He said that he shifted with no problem.

I could sense his great feeling of accomplishment as we sat in the kitchen at his mom's house having a beer.

He was talkative and bubbly, "I knew that guy was looking at my hook every time I had to shift. I could just feel his eyes watching me. I was afraid to look at him, I didn't know what he was going to say."

Pete, you sure did the right thing, I'm proud of you! It's been a long haul, but you made it!" I said, coming close to tears.

As his brothers and sisters came home from school, there was a lot of excited storytelling of how he knew how to make the proper turn onto one-way streets now. He was becoming a bit of a family hero, at long last.

I felt a warm glow inside for my friend who had made so much progress since that first night when he came to my house with a cast on his shortened arm. I felt there was no stopping him now. He was gradually regaining the confidence that was blown away that summer afternoon, three years before. Through his misfortune, I had gained a new friend.

Little did I know how valuable the experiences we had together over these years would be to me. Being an amputee - a person with one hand missing seemed to take on a new meaning.

CHAPTER 2

Building A Rocket Launcher

Pete and I had become the best of friends. More like buddies than father and son, I was about 15 years older than he. I began to live the world of an amputee, though the vicarious experiences with Pete. The more I thought about how life was with one hand, the more I liked the challenge of it. It was becoming obvious that missing a hand wasn't actually much of a "disability" if any at all. I could clearly see that it was the person's attitude that could be a problem and make life difficult while doing things with only one hand. True, activities would have to be done sometimes a bit differently, but the end result was about the same - especially if the person wanted to be successful at his endeavors. That "want" seemed to be the key to success as an amputee. Generally, when a person loses a limb he didn't want this to happen and is therefore unhappy with his amputee condition. This is the difference between an intentional BIID loss and an unexpected accidental one.

Pet's problem was that he didn't seem to be very confident, his self-worth feelings were fairly low. Thus he was easily discouraged from trying things because of his "disability. I didn't detect any negativism from his family or few friends, they seemed to be acceptive of his condition. His inability to get on with his life as a teen seemed to be the result of his outlook on life.

Eventually I decided that I too wanted to be a "one-hander." I was thoroughly convinced that being an amputee could actually be fun and quite a challenge and had no fears about it. I didn't think much about how my losing a hand would affect my friends or family, which I should have. My attitude was that if it wasn't a problem for me, so why would it bother them? Thus I put this aside and didn't give it much thought if any.

Could my childhood experience of seeing a one-hander at the supermarket have had any effect on my desire? It was a positive experience. I recall nothing that upset me or made me feel bad about seeing this amputee. Had it been a situation where I witnessed a traumatic accident, it probably would have left me with negative feelings about amputation. But my experience seeing this teen-age bag boy at the check out counter wasn't any thing unusual. He seemed to be performing his task of putting groceries into bags with out any problems, thus I had no reason to have any fears about being an amputee. It was different, but not bad.

Then the question arose, how? How could I get rid of my hand? What sort of accident could I contrive that would rid me of my hand and at the same time, satisfy any questions which might arise. A bomb blast was far too risky as this was Pete's experience. Not only did he loose his hand, but several fingers and thumb on his remaining hand. Besides, all of my friends knew I wasn't a pyro. As I ran through the various possibilities, I kept coming back to a table saw accident. I've been doing wood working all my life. I had a saw right there in my garage and it seemed the perfect method

With this in mind, I went to Sears and bought a new 10 blade, all sharp and shiny. No point in risking the whole thing on a used blade. I suppose my years of using the saw would put aside any questions about intentionally cutting off my hand on the saw, I should know what I'm doing. So I'd simply run it through the saw, then go to the hospital and have them sew me up.

One crisp, clear, Friday afternoon in February, Pete, his brothers and I went out into a field near my house to launch some of their solid-fuel rockets. Those guys were always trying something new. We had a small square of plywood that served as a launching pad. On top of this was mounted a small support stick which held the rocket and guided it as it was launched. The chemicals inside the rocket were ignited by a spark from a lantern battery. Inside the rocket was a little man with a parachute that was supposed to open and drop him back to earth. He often dropped straight down and crashed to earth with the spent rocket.

This was my first experience with solid fuel rockets. It was interesting to notice how high they went, almost out of sight. They often left a beautiful smoke trail that was soon bent by the prevailing winds into interesting white shapes against the clear blue winter sky. We tried to keep the missile in sight, so we could follow it down and recover it for another flight. These little rockets often lead us on quite a chase around the neighborhood, as they fell back to earth.

Pete usually was the one elected to do the risky work of launching, using his indestructible steel hook. I guess our theory was that a hand could only be blown off once, thus we took advantage of this, and Pete seemed to enjoy being considered special.

The launcher arm wasn't sturdy or long enough to properly support the missile on the launch pad, so I elected to design a better one the next morning. I told them I would have it ready when the guys came over the next day, or so this was going to be how I would tell them I had my "accident."

At last the time had come. I had thought and re-thought the "accident" process again and again, leaving little left to consider.

My workshop was the garage that was attached to my house. Even though it was the fourth of February, the weather was quite mild, perhaps 25 degrees, and clear. Inside the garage it was just above freezing, and a jacket and warm boots were necessary. For knocking around, I usually wore my fur-lined Eskimo-type boots, that were laced up with nylon cords. I never bothered to tie them up, it was too much work.

I always kept a good supply of odd pieces of wood around. It was often difficult to find a place to work with all the wood and unfinished projects in the single-stall garage.

Not having any one-inch wood stock on hand, I decided to use a length of two-by-four and cut it down to size. (Well, this is what I would tell everyone.) Before ripping it down to the desired thickness, it was easier to cut off the length I needed, then rip the shorter piece. The two-by-four was about ten feet long, and I needed about two feet of it. I've always preferred a table saw. It is possible to cut a full four-by-eight foot sheet of plywood on an open table saw, something that can't be done on a radial-arm saw. Also I never used the guard over the blade, as it just seemed to get in the way.

15

My story about how this all happened was to be that I stepped on my boot laces as I approached the saw with the long piece of wood, and tripped and fell into the whirring ten-inch saw blade, slicing off my hand in the process. I'd try to break my fall with my right arm, and in the process, it would strike the top of the table, and as I continued to fall forward, it would slide across the table and into the blade.

This was my "official" explanation as to how I cut off my hand, but here is how it really went; I was standing in front of that sharp whirling saw blade, at the point in my life when I was about to be a one-handed person. I was a bit jittery and nervous, but I wanted it very badly.

I may have stood there in front of the saw for as much as 15 minutes, working up the courage to do this, with all of these thoughts running through my head over and over. I needed to be sure I really wanted to do this Then I just did it. I pushed my arm through the saw blade somewhere just below my wrist. My determination was so strong that I went a bit too fast, and stalled the saw blade before it cut all the way through so I did it again, and again it stalled. This left me with two cuts through the bone with the hand still attached by connecting tissue. Well, It wasn't completely off, but I felt this was good enough.

I can remember my hand dangling from the end of my arm by a piece of skin. The blade went through my arm about an inch above the wrist and then closer to the wrist on the second attempt.

Thoughts whirred through my mind; "Heavy, heavy pain, just as if my funny bone was hit with a hammer. I'm bleeding." I applied pressure to the artery in my arm to stop it. "WOW I really cut my hand off The worst is now over. I have to turn off that noisy saw, I'll use my foot on the switch. How am I going to do anything if I have to keep holding pressure on my arm? Well, at least I'm not bleeding all over the place. Now to get to the hospital and let them finish it. Wait 'till Pete hears about this

Running an arm through a saw blade is not an easy thing to do, and I think I just wanted to "do it" and get it over with. In reality, I should have gone more slowly to allow the blade to cut through the bone. The motor wasn't strong enough for such a burst of heavy cutting.

I had several years experience in first aid so I knew that I had to control the bleeding above all else. I released the pressure long enough to go to the phone, put the receiver to my ear, and hold it with my shoulder, (as I often did anyway) and rotary dialed 0. I told the operator that this was an emergency, and I wanted to talk to the hospital. I asked for the emergency room. I told them who I was, what had happened, and who my doctor was. I said I'd be there in about ten minuets. Then I told the operator to ring my friend Todd, who lived just behind me on the next street. (This was back in the days when you could actually talk to an operator in your own town.)

Hello Todd, come over quick, I cut my hand and I need you to take me to the hospital.

I told Todd that I cut my hand, but not off . I didn't want to shake him up over the phone. I tried to sort things through in my mind, WOW What a heavy ache. I've bumped my funny bone before, but never had an ache as heavy as this I feel so good that it's finally over with, what a relief.

Todd arrived in a flash, he lived behind me, he must have ran full-speed all the way over.

I thought you just cut your finger or something, you didn't say you cut your whole hand off, WOW " he said breathlessly.

I know, but I didn't want to get you all excited. The keys to the van are in my coat pocket here, on the left side. We'd better wrap my hand and arm in that white towel, it's pretty clean.

It was strange not to be able to feel my hand, as we put the towel around it. It was just dead weight, attached by some skin to my arm. It was the arm that had plenty of feeling left in it

We gently made our way out to the van with Todd carrying my lifeless hand wrapped in the towel and me following, as we were still connected. I maintained the pressure on the artery to control the bleeding. We tried to move together as one, so that we didn't stretch the connecting section of skin. I sat on the seat in front, and we gently placed the towel and hand in my lap. The hand was beginning to feel mentally more apart from my body, as I sat there thinking about it. In the back of my mind I was hoping that they wouldn't attempt to re-attach it. Taking it to the hospital with me was just a formality.

Todd jumped in the drivers seat and we took off. The hospital was only about five miles from my house. Todd's foot on the gas pedal was shaking. I think he was more upset by all this than I was. Well, I knew what was going on and how I felt, he didn't.

You don't have to drive so fast, I said, It's alright. I'm not bleeding to death.

And I don't even have my driver's license yet, he said with a tight quivering voice.

Well, I'm sure they'll overlook that if we get stopped. We could probably drive a hundred miles an hour, and never get stopped, now that we have a real emergency I joked. We both got a good laugh out of that possibility.

I wonder now, some 35 years later, how Todd would react if he knew the true story that I did it intentionally. I have told only one person in my circle of friends and family back then, that I did it because I wanted to be an amputee. This sort of thing just isn't done. Only a crazy person would do this Even today I have reservations about coming out with my true story. The world can be very lonely when your friends don't want to have anything to do with you because they think you're nuts. I guess I feel that it's been some 35 years since I did it, and I really have nothing to hide. I'm not a criminal and have been a useful, successful person since. If someone can't accept this, then I probably don't need them as a friend. It's the only way I can justify telling the world.

I revealed my deed to friends in later life when the first printing of this book came out in 2002. I lived in a small town in southern Oregon. Word gets around fast in small towns - what else is there to talk about? As I look back on this period, it seems the more educated people took it in stride. They had known me for a few years and knew I was a sane, rational person. I was active in the community and was quite successful. Crazy people aren't usually this successful. Others who didn't know me personally or who had minimal education shunned me. This seems to be the way it works.

At the hospital the emergency staff was waiting for us as we pulled up to the entrance. They placed me on a table and arranged a support on the right side for my arm. A tourniquet was placed on my arm as someone took down my name, address, and other usual admittance information. At last I could release the pressure that I was maintaining to control the bleeding. My left hand was almost paralyzed from maintaining its' grip. I guess I was subconsciously trying not to let myself bleed to death. Now I could relax and let someone competent do what was necessary. I was also ready for something to ease the pain. I still had a super-heavy, dull ache in my arm. That's what it felt like to have a hand cut off.

After taking my blood pressure, the nurse remarked that it was good. Evidently I was successful and hadn't lost much blood. I had 2 years training in first-aid by directing the televising of first-aid college courses at the university where I worked. The importance of the control of bleeding was thoroughly drummed into my head and this proved how important it is.

As I lie there, I was afraid to move my arm, even the slightest bit. I didn't even try to look at it. I decided to let them attend to it. There wasn't much I could do at this point, I just wanted to relax and take it easy and I felt very calm inside - partly because of the medication they gave me, partly because I was on the edge of being a one-handed person at last Details were becoming fuzzy, this was so good

My doctor called in an orthopedic surgeon because of the possibility of reconnecting my hand. When the specialist arrived, he assessed the situation. Because my arm was cut through twice. it would have been very difficult to successfully reconnect all the nerves (this was 35 years ago) He said it would be doubtful that the hand would ever become functional and have feeling. If it wasn't successful, I'd probably have to have it taken off later anyway. Fortunately for me it seemed very doubtful that he could save the hand. I quietly breathed a sigh of relief. With a useless hand, I couldn't ride my bike, hold a ski pole, row a boat, or pitch hay as Pete could. No thanks I felt I'd still be able to do everything I ever did before. I knew Pete could, if he'd let himself...

Yes, I said to the orthopedic surgeon, You might as well finish what I started. Little did he know the truth in this statement.

An elderly nurse took me up to the operating room. she was a nice lady. (In my condition, however, anyone probably would have seemed nice.) She was very gentle and reassuring. Her attitude was very comforting to me. Because my folks were out of town for the weekend, and it all happened so fast, I didn't have the moral support of anyone I knew, at a time when

I needed it most. I was probably with her only a few minutes, but I will remember her forever.

Instead of a general anesthetic, they gave me a nerve-block. I had eaten breakfast that morning, as I always do, and they told me there was a possibility that I might throw up while under the anesthetic and choke. The anesthetist inserted a tube into an artery in my neck to administer the drugs. Then we all waited for them to take effect. As I lay on the table, waiting for the pain to go away, the doctor fiddled with the tubes that ran down my neck and inside of me. We waited some more. They probably all got bored, and decided to prepare for the surgery while waiting.

As I lay there, I considered the events of that morning, I felt elated I did it I did it I felt pretty lucky, everything went as planned, and the worst was now over.

At last the operation proceeded, but I was still waiting for the anesthetic to take effect. A tent-like partition was erected on my right side, between me and the activity at the end of my arm. I couldn't see what was being done, but I could sure feel it.

The surgeon began by sawing off a small section of bone from the end of my arm. The bones of my forearm had to be shortened so that there was enough skin remaining to cover the end of the arm. Then he neatly filed the ends of the bones to round the edges.

It was then that I experienced the most intense pain that I have ever felt in my life. It's a good thing they gave me the nerve-block, or it would have been really bad, but it couldn't have been much worse The best way I can describe the pain is, white hot. The anesthetist made the comment that I probably thought I was back in the middle ages, before the use of pain killers and I whole-heartedly agreed.

The doctors talked about skiing conditions last weekend. Idle chit-chat was exchanged while he sewed up the end of my arm, pulling a flap of skin over the end of the bone that he neatly rounded off. The thicker the padding of skin at the end of the arm, the more comfortable it is when one has to put pressure on the arm to get up, etc.

Winters in the north are long and hard. I always looked forward to the first snowfall and the prospect of skiing. I had been skiing for almost ten years at the time I met Pete. I'm not an aggressive person, thus it took me longer to learn to parallel ski than most people. Most of my friends in our town of 12,000 people were skiers too.

I eventually got Pete interested in skiing. We talked at length about how he would be able to grasp a ski pole with his hook. When he tried one of mine, it just dangled at the end of his arm. He couldn't plant it where he wanted to. In order for the pole to be useful, Pete had to have a reasonable amount of control over it or it wouldn't be worth using. Many one-armed skiers use only one pole, but we felt two would give Pete an extra bit of stability and balance. A firmer grip was necessary, however.

We spent a lot of time in Pete's basement, experimenting with several types of rubber grips. Eventually we settled on a motorcycle handle grip with a large metal washer mounted at its' base. The hand grip was the plastic type that was puffed up with air inside. With the washer mounted on the pole at the base of the grip, he could exert downward pressure on the pole. The soft surface of the grip allowed the opening of the farmer's hook to sink into it, providing a firmer grip. This seemed to be an effective yet rather simple solution to his pole problem.

Thirty years later I finally came across a good device for holding a ski pole. It's basically a block of flexible rubber with a hole in it. This rubber has a stud sticking out of it which screws into the end of the prosthesis. The end of the ski pole rod is forced up into the hole which holds it firmly. The rubber allows the pole to flex forward as the skier goes to plant the pole in the snow while skiing. It works quite well. I personally like using two poles, as it's always there if you need to catch yourself for balance. With out it, you can fall down, it's that simple.

Pete soon became a very tough and aggressive skier. I had a hard time keeping up with him, even with my years of skiing experience. Skiing was an excellent outlet that allowed Pete to show us all that he could indeed excel and go as far as he would let himself. The only real problem that we encountered was the cold. His prosthesis was made of a hard fiberglass material. It was insulated from his skin with a thick sock, which was made especially to fit his arm size. After four or five hours of being out in the twenty-degree weather, his arm became stone cold. It even ached after a while. There were several cracked and broken skis that winter, but it was well worth it in terms of enjoyment and feelings of accomplishment. Pete learned to ski after he lost his hand.

I thought about all of this as I laid there in the operating room. There shouldn't be any reason for me to have any trouble skiing, I already knew how We were going to go up skiing the next week-end, and I decided to go along with my friends, but it would be a while before I could use both poles again but I could still take pictures of the other guys as we had planed.

As the surgeon finished with the sutures, he left a rubber drainage tube called a "shunt" in place. It would have to remain sticking out of the wound for a few days to allow excess body fluid to drain, and preventing swelling.

I was afraid to even try to flex the muscles in my arm. The slightest attempt was very painful. It was going to be interesting to try to move my fingers (the muscles in the arm that used to be attached to the fingers, that is). I wondered what it would feel like. I decided to leave well enough alone, for the time being. I just wanted sleep...

As I drifted in and out of dreamland, I remember my friend Joyce at my side in the hospital room. She lived next door when I was in high school. Out families are still close friends, although we live apart. Now, thirteen years later, she was a nurse in this very hospital. It was comforting to have a close friend at my side. Although I wasn't very coherent at times throughout the afternoon, we talked about activities we both enjoyed. We had skied together, and eventually got around to the subject. I told her how my friend Pete and I hassled with his pole problem and that we finally got it worked out. I said I didn't think it would be any big problem for me either. She didn't know Pete and our relationship and she wasn't aware of my experiences with this one-hander, so was a bit uncertain about my rather resilient composure so soon after my traumatic experience. She had difficulty understanding how I could take such a tragic loss so lightly and later she said she didn't think I was really aware of what happened. Thirty years later, I gave Joyce a copy of the first printing of this book to read. She took it in stride as I thought she would. She made the comment that she thought I was in denial about the whole affair, because I didn't seem to be devastated by the fact that I just lost my right hand. Now she understood why I was in such a good mood in my hospital bed. We're still good friends.

When I awoke late that afternoon, I began to think about the days events, So this is what it feels like to have a hand missing My arm is so light without the weight of the hand on the end of it. I wonder what they did with it? It was perfectly good Didn't I just cut my fingernails the day before? I guess it could be preserved in a jar of formaldehyde, but that would be gross. It feels like my arm is spring-loaded. It wants to pop up, all by itself. I suppose the forearm muscles are accustomed to having two or three pounds of hand weight at the end of it. Now without it, they are unbalanced. I wonder if the steel hook and plastic arm like Pete has, will compensate and keep it down?"

Now I know that the prosthetic arm is quite a bit heavier than the hand it replaces. It can even get tiresome at the end of a long day of working with it.

"I'll have to move it slowly and carefully," I thought, "it's so sensitive and tender right now. It hurts, but nothing like this morning when they were operating. I suppose the worst of the pain is over...

By dinner that night I was pretty hungry, I didn't have anything to eat since breakfast. When the food came, I dove in. I quickly found that I couldn't eat as much as I thought I could but it sure tasted good however, and I got to choose my menus for the next day

My parents were out of town for the weekend and didn't know about all this. I called several friends on the phone while lying in bed. They said later that I sounded a bit shook, but otherwise in good spirits. I knew I had to be careful not to reveal how happy I was about this whole affair. They wouldn't understand this anyway.

Experiencing the reaction of my friends for the first time was often as uncomfortable for me as it was for them. Some of them didn't know how to react to my situation. They weren't aware of my prior experience with Pete which had pre-conditioned me to life with one hand. Because they felt uncomfortable about my condition, I too felt awkward in their presence. This happens often between amputees and friends who have difficulty dealing with their loss. As the amputee becomes more comfortable with their own condition, these feelings are picked up by friends, and they too feel more at ease. My friends often felt sorrow and remorse over my loss. My feelings were more of anticipation of a new way of life, rather than fear of the unknown.

As I was well aware of the many problems encountered by this type of loss, I often joked about my condition when friends came to visit me. Many of them said later that they thought I wasn't fully aware of the seriousness of my accident, and wasn't accepting it - what else could they think?

I didn't sleep well the first night, I woke up frequently. A nurse gave me a hypo to ease the pain and relax me. I found I had to sleep on my back with my arm on a pillow, I didn't dare move too much. This was the most comfortable position I could find. Heaven forbid, should I roll over on my shorter arm, the whole orthopedic ward would hear about it

The sensitivity of the cut nerve endings gradually became less and less. In about two or three weeks, the pain was mostly gone except when the area was bumped or pressed, then pain could be felt. Occasionally people experience lasting feelings that a hand or limb is still there, but it's not painful. This is my case. I can still feel my fingers move, bit it's not painful.

When my friend Bill came to see me the next day, he asked me how I slept. I told him I had a wristless night. He said later he knew I'd be all right. I've never told Bill the truth. I think he'd have difficulty accepting this, even though we're the best of friends. I think I'll leave well enough alone. Telling the truth is often much harder than getting along with one hand - that's the easy part.

My folks were quite tense when they arrived Sunday night. Mom especially, I could tell by the grim expression on her face. She felt a lot better when she found me in good spirits. Here was her child in the hospital after losing his hand All the struggles and hardships that were overcome raising her children down through the years, and now this

I could almost read her mind; What will become of him now? Will he have to find

easier work? Will he ever drive again? He was such an active boy, water skiing, motorcycling and playing bass guitar in a band. What a devastating blow I could sense her anguish, but never told her the truth. She didn't know Pete and didn't have the insight I had. Inwardly I felt bad about this deception. I didn't intend to hurt her. This is one of the side effects that didn't occur to me when I planned this whole affair. I suppose it was because I had confidence about the outcome and she didn't.

What a big moment when Pete and his family came to see me in the hospital for the first time I expected him to laugh his ass off, but he managed to maintain his composure. I was sure he must have been thinking something like, Revenge at last

His dad seemed the most hurt by it all. I could sense his feelings of sorrow that I to had to go through this, just as he did with his son. Pete seemed a bit puzzled by my rather jovial mood. He was reluctant to joke with me. I didn't press the issue as I understood the conflicting thoughts that he must have been feeling. His accident and loss hurt him very badly. I was in a good mood and this didn't make sense.

By Monday I was ready to climb the walls, and single-handedly too My arm still hurt a lot, but otherwise I was feeling rather good, all things considered. I was getting bored, despite the fact that I had more books than I could ever read, thanks to my friends. I was ready to go home and pick up where I left off (except for my rocket launcher project).

My doctor agreed to let me go home Monday afternoon. I was to come back at the end of the week so he could check my progress. It would be several weeks before the stitches would come out. He assured me that I'd be fitted with a new arm in no time at all That was the best news I had since the decision to use a nerve block for pain relief The nerve block was a big failure, but I knew that using a prosthesis was no problem. I actually had a lot to look forward to. What a huge difference in outlook compared to most people who loose a limb. This is what people don't know about or understand with BIID. Losing a hand for us is a very positive event. I know this sounds strange, but it's the way it is.

I was in and out of the hospital in three days and felt pretty good. For some however, the pain and suffering seems endless.

In the years since, I've talked to a few others who cut off their hand on purpose, and they can't say exactly why they did it. It seems to be a desire buried deep in the subconscious somewhere. It drives us for unknown reasons. This is the big mystery surrounding BIID. Why would any one want to do such a thing Even the BIID'ers themselves don't seem to know for sure. Perhaps by the time you finish this book, you'll be able to identify why I did it

CHAPTER 3

More Than A Hand

It was a clear night, the stars were like diamonds in the black northern sky. The cool June air had a rich, fresh, forest smell. This was Northern Wisconsin logging country.

Tom was heading home from a friend's house where he helped put a transmission in a car. Tom was quite a mechanical wizard. He lived outside of town on a farm with his family. He just finished his junior year in high school. Tom was one of those good-looking, well built football heros. He sacked twenty-three himself in one game. He ran a lot and lifted weights to stay in shape. His dream was to continue on to college playing football.

It was nearly ten-thirty. Only one more payment and his 750cc three-cylinder bike was all his. It had plenty of guts. If he wasn't careful, it could flip over backwards if he opened it up. A friend who had helped him work on the car, wanted a ride home. Tom said he couldn't, he didn't have another helmet.

On the highway, he passed a slow car, heading down a hill, just before the bridge over the Menominee River that separates Wisconsin from Upper Michigan. After getting back into his lane, he noticed a car across the center of the road ahead of him, under the street light.

What the hell is he doing parked there? Tom said to himself.

He started to go around to the left, to cross in front of the car. At that same instant, the car started to move forward. Tom thought the driver was going to floor it to get out of the way, so he swerved to the right to go

26

behind the car. Instead of continuing to move out of Tom's way, the car suddenly stopped again.

Smucko-o, I hit the rear end of the car, just behind the left wheel. Something told me to stiffen-up and turn my head, he later remembered. My left arm was driven through the rear side window and into the back one, smashing the glass out. The car was spun around by the force of the impact.

Tom was taken by ambulance to the hospital in Iron Mountain, just a few miles away. When his parents arrived, the doctors advised them to have him taken down to Green Bay, 100 miles to the south. His injuries appeared too numerous and severe to be handled with their limited resources. There was even some doubt that he would survive the trip. He was in pretty bad shape.

Tom's mother rode in the front of the ambulance, and recalled the trip;

It was a beautiful moonlit night, deer were all over the road. I helped the driver watch for them. He'd turn on the siren and spotlight to scare them off the road. We made the trip in one hour and ten minutes.

Tom was in surgery for over nine hours. He was bleeding internally and needed nine pints of blood. The nerves in his left arm were ripped apart at the shoulder, where he had a broken breast bone. His left wrist was fractured. He had a broken right femur and his right wrist had a compound fracture. He also had a ruptured spleen and bruised kidney. The doctors gave him less than a fifty-fifty chance to live.

He was young and strong, I thought he'd make it, but it would be rough, his mom said. I kept talking to him in the emergency room. I had nurse's training. They told us that unconscious people often hear, so I thought I might somehow give him some strength. The priest and doctors there didn't think he'd make it.

The doctors spent four hours setting broken bones, and one-and-a-half hours just re-connecting the severed artery to his left arm. They put casts on both arms, leaving just his fingers sticking out, and a full length cast on his right leg.

Tom was in a coma for over two-and-a-half weeks, often drifting in and out of semi-consciousness.

At last he opened his eyes, Hi Mom...What's wrong with my arm? he asked.

You hit the side of a car, she explained. The nerves in your shoulder were pulled apart. They couldn't re-attach them to the spinal column. Some opposite ends couldn't be found.

Due to the severity of his many other injuries, the doctors and specialists did the best they could for his arm, within the time available, in order to save his life.

I remember passing the car, but not hitting one, he managed to say.

At night, while lying in his hospital bed, Tom often had dreams, while under the influence of the pain-killing drugs. A pin that held his leg in traction was bent one night while he thrashed around. The doctor told him that it wouldn't hurt when he began to turn the hand drill to insert a new pin. Tom's screams could be heard all over the eighth floor.

Ironically, only a few weeks before the accident, Tom saw a young girl gymnast perform on TV. She had only one arm.

I felt sorry for her at the time, and thought how rough it must have been for her. A neighbor girl lost her hand when she was only two. If they could make it, so could I. I may not have the use of my left arm, but I sure can have a strong right, he decided.

The neurologist could not promise that the feeling would return to his lifeless left arm. The fact that it had

stabbing pains at times promised some hope. Time would tell.

Tom had been in bed, flat on his back for six weeks. All of his former strength had drained out of him. The first time he was allowed out of bed to stand, his left leg was like rubber. He lost so much weight, that the nurses at his side had to hold up the shorts that his mom brought him to wear.

He was really, really thin, his mother recalled. By the seventh week he was walking. He had to have his left shoe built up because of the thick cast on his right leg. It was good exercise for him to haul the sixty pounds of plaster around.

Before the accident, Tom was very active. He helped with the farm work and always had some kind of project going. He welded, laid cement at his brother's new house and tinkered with cars and bikes. The forced rest in the hospital, combined with the prospect of not ever regaining the use of his left arm, caused him to think about what he was going to do in the future.

It really turned my life around. Sometimes you get off in the wrong direction. I had time to think about the things I did, much more than I ever had before. That was one good thing that came out of it all. Our family had some rough times, and this brought us all of us closer together. An accident as serious as mine made a lot of every-day problems seem silly in comparison. I was lucky just to be alive.

Most people with extensive injuries such as Tom's would have been in a hospital for at least six months. Tom returned to the farm after only seven weeks Few people recover from basilary skull fractures, such as Tom's, without being paralyzed from the neck down.

He was getting around with the aid of a crutch that had a support for his broken wrist. When he got home, he headed for the garage to see what was left of his bike.

I took one look at it lying there and just shook my head. I made my last payment on it and it was just a twisted mass. I figured I could make a go-cart out of the engine anyway, he said with a sigh.

As he was going up the steps to the house for the first time, his crutch slipped and he banged his pinned right wrist. When he got in the kitchen, he noticed some movement inside the cast.

The next morning when I woke up, I couldn't believe the pain in my wrist. The pins holding the bones together were bent, so it was back to Green Bay again, he remembered.

With so much nursing experience in the family, the most logical thing to do was to set up a hospital bed right there in the living room, his mother related. That way we wouldn't have to climb the stairs to his bedroom. Then we could all take care of him. He was so weak he couldn't do anything for himself. With the cast on his right arm with just his fingers sticking out, he couldn't even lift a half-gallon of milk or feed himself.

The familiar surroundings of his family and friends were a tremendous boost to Tom's morale. His accident and the loss of the use of his left arm was well accepted by his family. Though he certainly was treated with tender loving care, he was also made to feel that he could do as much as he wanted to do, within the limitations of his physical condition. They didn't talk about what he wouldn't be able to do now, with only one useful arm. Instead, they all sought new ways for Tom to accomplish the things he did before the accident. Actually, Tom didn't need much help with his innate, eager and positive disposition, it was difficult to hold him back.

He was home by himself most of the day. His mother was teaching school, his dad was working as a service man for the farm co-op, and his brothers and sisters were off to school. After his first week at home, he was able to feed himself, and was soon out walking. He would trudge over to his sister's new home, several blocks down the road, hauling his heavy plaster arm and leg casts with him. It was a long, slow walk, but was exactly the sort of exercise he needed. This also gave him plenty of time to reflect on his direction in life.

Living back at home, away from the safe hospital environment wasn't always easy. One night, the family was woken by the sound of Tom screaming from outside the house. The wild dreams he had during his sleep at night, which were caused by the medications he had taken to ease the pain over the past two months, were continuing. It seems Tom had somehow gotten out of bed during one of these dreams and had wandered out of the house. He had fallen down the back stairs into the yard. His toes, which stuck out of the end of his leg cast, were nearly broken of by the weight of the heavy plaster as he toppled over and down the steps to the back entrance. It seemed as if his pain would never end.

His arm casts came off in September, the leg cast in October. Getting rid of all that dead weight was a tremendous feeling. they were a constant source of irritation. His limbs inside the cast were always in need of scratching. he had difficulty applying enough pressure with the end of a fly swatter because of the cast on his only good hand. He often had one of his brothers or sisters scratch for him. Now, one more of his burdens was over. The casts came off just in time for Tom to be the best man at his brother's wedding. The family now had two big events to celebrate

Tom returned to school the fourth week of November, after hunting season. This was his senior year. There was much work to be made up, but his first semester was relatively light. He had two hours of gym class scheduled. He would work out on the bench press, doing ten repetitions with 225 pounds. The best he could start with now, was forty pounds. He eventually worked his way up to one-thirty-five, with one arm

The second semester Tom had eight classes. He did have problems in math class. Not with the subject, but with the teacher. The recurring pains in his paralyzed left arm, which he carried in a sling, were a constant irritation. If he was able to keep his mind active and away from his arm, he usually wasn't aware of the pain. While sitting in a quiet classroom, however, his mind would often drift back to his arm and the pains would return. Sometimes he had to get up and walk around or leave the room. He said the pain would drive him up the wall. They were sharp, sometimes stabbing, and would come and go without warning. Unfortunately, there was little that could be done for them. This is a common occurrence with nerve damage.

Because of this, he had a permanent pass from the principal for leaving classes. His math teacher couldn't understand this problem. He didn't realize that Tom didn't want to sit in class among his fellow students, with his face distorted in pain. The teacher couldn't understand what walking around had to do with pains in his arm.

Tom got an A-plus in speech that semester. His talk centered around his accident, a subject that he was all too familiar with. He referred to it as a living hell, to be bound by heavy casts, in traction and to suffer stabbing pains. The pains would often shoot down his arm and explode in his hand. For an arm without feeling, it sure raised a lot of hell Tom recalled.

Socially, carrying his arm in a sling was no problem at all. Now the girls would come up to him and strike up conversations. He had a personality that would win them over, his mother remembered. If only he could keep his mind off his arm, life would have been easier, and less painful.

Thinking about wild women was a tremendous outlet, Tom remembered with a smile. His girl friend often came over to his house to console him. He had known her since seventh grade. She thought of him as a Walking Miracle.

Tom's neck bothered him while in school when he spent a lot of time looking down at books and papers. This strained the damaged vertebra in his neck and back. Sitting down for long periods of time was especially difficult.

Tom felt bad that he couldn't play football this last year in school. He walked into the locker room one afternoon, to visit.

The coach said, Here comes the all-conference noseguard It almost brought tears to Tom's eyes. He often thought of going on to college on a football scholarship. There was not much chance of that now.

Tom's auto mechanics class gave him a chance to learn and practice the theory behind what he had been doing for many years at home. His shop teacher said that he couldn't believe some of the things he was accomplishing with only one hand; changing points, timing the ignition, even taking a rear-end apart with no problems at all. Grinding valves involved two operations at the same time. Tom would turn a knob on the grinding machine with his knee, while rotating another with his right hand.

When you have only one hand to work with, you become very creative. I use just about any method that works. I use my leg, knee and even feet, in place of a second hand, to steady or hold things, he chuckled. When I work on an engine, I really get my whole body into it. You can't worry about what it might look like to other people, if you are going to get the job done. I use my two knees a lot, to hold things when I work on them. A vise on a bench is just about the best tool I can think of. It really takes the place of my other hand, and it isn't all that bad when you start to get into it. I do the same work as other people, but it might take a little longer, and I might go about it a little differently. I get the same results in the end.

Tom got an all-school award that year that said he could do more with one hand than most people could with two. Once he set his mind to do something, he'd find some way of doing it.

The summer that Tom graduated from high school, he peeled and skidded pulp wood - with one arm. It was steadily regaining its former strength. He'd try to lift increasingly larger logs, testing himself each time, to see just how much he could accomplish in order to determine his limitations. He would do push-ups with his right hand in a fist, because it would no longer bend at the wrist. he often joked that a stiff wrist was better than no wrist at all

I came close to losing my right hand, he recalled, That wrist was in pretty bad shape, but my mom and sister soaked it a lot and pulled it through. I've got to build up my right arm. It is the only one I've got to work with, so it might as well be as strong as possible.

Tom could do just about anything he wanted to; It just takes a little bit more consideration and forethought. I've always got my two feet and teeth to use if necessary, he said in a light-hearted mood.

I always thought nothing could hurt me. I felt strong and confident, but I found out different. I've always wanted to have the strength to do what ever I wanted to. The other day I snapped off a half-inch bolt working on my car. I'm getting stronger. I used to be impatient. The accident forced me to slow down and think more about what I'm doing. I've cried several times, thinking about my useless arm, and wondering if it would ever come back. I can feel it when it gets really cold out. The chiropractor said if there is pain, there is still some hope. The pain isn't as bad as it used to be. It began to die down after a year or so. I move my arm to keep the joints free. The doctor says it isn't a decision that has to be made now, but the arm will probably have to go, but I think it's going to come back, after the good lord gets me where he wants me. I just take one day at a time...

Tom attended technical school, studying mechanical design and drafting, taking advantage of his interest and background in mechanics.

The fact that Tom was able to use only one arm was not a problem for him. It was more often, a problem for those that did not know him and his natural abilities and resourcefulness. For Tom, losing the use of his arm did not mean the end of a useful existence - it was a new challenge.

During his second year in technical school, Tom did not return home one evening. Several days later his car was found in a swamp just off the road, not far from his home, by a farm neighbor. Little is known about what happened, except that he evidently died instantly in the crash.

CHAPTER 4

Back To Work

Tuesday was my first real day back in the world as a "one-hander". I woke up in my very own bed, in a room that was familiar for a change. The room was the same, but I felt strangely different. I was afraid to move my right arm. If I didn't, it generally felt alright. However, if I did the wrong thing with it, bumped it, or accidently tried to move a finger (which wasn't there anymore) or thought of flexing my wrist, (which was also gone) I would experience some very intense, sharp pains. I tried to avoid this situation at all costs. Otherwise, there was usually a low-level, constant ache. I had the arm cushioned on a pillow at my side throughout the night. This I found to be the most comfortable position. I often thought how this was a lot better than if I had lost a leg. Then I'd really have a problem taking care of myself alone. Some years later I asked several different types of amputees if they'd rather lose a leg or an arm. It was interesting that those who lost a leg said they'd rather have lost an arm than a leg. Those who had lost an arm said they'd rather have lost a leg. Apparently each had adjusted to their loss and viewed the other as a much more difficult condition to deal with. It seems to be a matter of individual adjustment.

It was now time to get up and face the world. I'd procrastinated long enough. I headed for the bathroom. What a strange feeling to urinate using one hand rather than two! I had never given this much thought before. I suppose most men use two hands, it seemed the natural thing to do. It was as if it wouldn't work with only one hand.

I carefully put a plastic bag over my bandaged stump, and secured it with a rubber band. I wasn't instructed to do this before I left the hospital, it just seemed a logical thing to do. In the shower, washing under my right arm was no problem. I found, however, that I had to flex my wrist as far as it would go with the soap in my hand, in order to get under my left armpit. It was a bit difficult and awkward at first, but it worked O.K.

To shampoo my hair, I had to hold the bottle against my side with my right elbow, and open the top, tipping the bottle enough to pour a small quantity into my hand, while holding the cap in my fingers. then I had to screw the cap back on the bottle without letting the shampoo run out of my cupped hand. I have since switched to a shampoo that has a flip-top, which is much easier.

I then found that I had to revise my usual method of drying with a towel. I was no longer able to pull the towel back and forth across my back with a corner in each hand. I found it necessary to flip it over my back and draw it up several times.

Dressing myself was awkward at first. I had to pull my pants up using a left-right-left-right pull, until they were all the way up. Tucking in the shirt took longer. I went round and round till it was all in, while still trying to keep the pants up. Then I could tighten the belt.

I never thought about the routine of putting on my socks before. I usually pulled with both hands, one on each side of the sock. I found that one hand works well, after the foot is worked into the sock. I wasn't about to hassle with shoe laces, so I put on my boots. Now I can easily tie laces with one hand when I don't use my hook during the heat of the summer. It is a matter of positioning the laces on top of the shoe and being rather clever with finger manipulations. I decided one day that I had to tie them when I didn't have my arm on, and was too lazy to put it on just to tie my shoes. It is the old story of necessity. I decided then that I'd take a few minutes and figure out how to do it. It wasn't hard, it just required a bit of specific effort. This was another task that could have taught me in some sort of a "rehabilitation school" but I was anxious to get on with my life, so I solved these little problems as I encountered them.

It took longer to button my shirt. I had to wrestle with each button, fishing it though the hole with one hand. When I finally got to the top of the shirt, I found one side higher than the other, and had to start all over again! I rolled the sleeve of my short arm up several times, then kept it in place with a rubber band. Now some 35 years later, I think I own only one shirt with buttons. Buttons are just not worth the effort!

By the time I got dressed, I was quite hungry. I found I had to make several trips to the breakfast table from the fridge, carrying one item at a time. It wasn't long before I began to use my foot for things like closing the door as I turned to the table with food.

Previously I would have held a box of cereal in my right hand while opening it with the left. I soon found it best to set the box down on the table before attempting to open it. Many years of experience have taught me that it isn't worth the effort to close the boxes tightly with he cardboard flaps tucked in perfectly.

While I'm on the subject of opening boxes and packages of various kinds of food, this may be a good time to vent my frustration over the new indestructible inner plastic bags found in most cereal boxes. I can never get the damn things open! The plastic material is so strong that one hand and even a hook cannot pull them apart where they are sealed at the top. What ever happened to the old-fashioned wax paper bags? They were a breeze!

Next, I found I had to put the jar of jam on the floor between my feet to hold it tight enough to unscrew the lid. I am now careful to screw lids of all types on very lightly; you might say, "one hand tight".

Chasing a piece of toast around the table with a butter knife wasn't much fun, as it got cold. It was necessary to "corner" it against something like a bread board, spreading toward the board, to keep it from sliding away. Later, when I got my hook, the hook could then steady the toast, anywhere I chose to butter it. When I got to the bottom of the bowl of cereal, I couldn't tip it up, in order to get the last few spoons full. I found it was easier to tip the bowl right into my mouth, and forget the spoon. This technique may not be proper etiquette, but it gets the job done.

Doing dishes with one hand was a trick at first. I chased the dishes around in the sink with one hand and a sponge. If I could corner a glass to keep it in place, I could get the sponge down inside of it. Now when I do dishes in the summer, when I'm not wearing my prosthesis, I can stick my arm right down inside the glass and run it around, instead of using a sponge held by my hook.

When the doctor asked me how I was doing when I next saw him, I said I had a hassle doing dishes with one hand, but otherwise was doing fine. He smiled with a rather strange expression on his face, as if this wasn't supposed to be my problem. It was the worst one I could think of at the time.

This was the seventh of February. In the north, this means warm clothing was the order of the day. I gently slid my right arm into the coat sleeve. I tucked the empty end of the sleeve into the right pocket to keep it from flopping around and to keep cold air from going up the sleeve. It also seemed that it would look better to have it in the pocket, rather than hanging empty from my shoulder. One couldn't tell that I didn't have a hand on the end of my arm if the sleeve was in my pocket. I thought this was pretty sneaky. I wasn't totally at ease in public and I was beginning to understand why Pete felt uncomfortable venturing out into the world after his accident. Now it was my turn to experience this phenomenon.

Going to work, I went out through the garage and passed the table saw. My friends did a nice job of cleaning things up while I was gone. Not a trace of blood was to be found. I felt rather unbalanced as I lifted the garage door to go out. I never realized that I probably used two hands to raise the door previously.

With the key in my left hand, I found the ignition switch was now on the wrong side of the steering column. I reached around and under the wheel to insert the key. This irritating problem hasn't change a bit over the years. For a left-hander, right-hand ignition switches just don't work well.

I had the habit of steering with one hand as long as I could remember, so this wouldn't be a problem. The transmission was automatic. I moved the lever by reaching over the wheel. Pressing down on the gas, I was off to my first day at work with one hand!

I operated the TV Production Studio at a large technical school. With 3,000 students enrolled, this would not be a good place for a person to work if he felt self-conscious. When my supervisor came to visit me in the hospital, I asked him if he would spread the word about my accident, so I wouldn't have to go through the explanation again and again. This strategy seemed to work. It relieved me of having to deal with the surprise and subsequent expressions of sympathy of those who hadn't heard about it at all. Also, being that I wasn't telling the whole truth about my accident, I felt a bit uneasy telling my ""fib" every time.

Having known Pete and his difficulties after his accident, helped me to cope with meeting people for the first time with a bandage ball at the end of my arm. I didn't mind all the questions, it just got to be a hassle after a while with so many people in school. I didn't accomplish much that first day, I mostly put in an appearance. I went home that afternoon when the stabbing pains returned.

The pains were intermittent. It wasn't long before I realized that the more I consciously thought about my arm, the more intense the pain became. When I was engrossed in my work, I seldom noticed the pain. With severe, prolonged cases of pain, a series of cortisone shots are sometimes given directly into the limb. Occasionally a condition known as neuroma occurs. The nerves in the stump attempt to regenerate, growing into tiny balls, causing intense pain. These balls can be surgically removed if necessary. Fortunately I didn't have this problem.

I occasionally took an empirin number three compound, a prescription for severe pain. These weren't very effective against sharp pains, however. These stabbing pains reoccurred with lessening frequency for about two or three months. Eventually they subsided altogether. Amputees experience pain in differing amounts and durations. It depends upon the amount of nerve damage and how the nerve ends heal.

Some have what is often referred to as "phantom limb sensations," not necessarily pains, but feeling that the lost hand or fingers are still there. I can still feel the wiggle of my fingers or count on them, through these sensations. The feeling is as if the hand and fingers are moving, but without the feeling of touch. The delicate surface sensations of the finger tips are absent. Only the inner movement feeling remains.

The nerves that once went to my fingers are still there in my arm, and remain sensitive to these feelings. I often entertain myself by tapping my fingers secretly inside my arm, and no one ever knows it! My first day was as a one-handed person went well. I had no bad experiences and felt as though I'd be able to continue my job as it was before with few problems.

Wednesday I took the day off and drove with Todd in my van to visit my grandparents. They lived about sixty miles north. The drive gave us a chance to reflect on the events of the past few days. After my short day at work, I began to sense that my life was going to be just fine.

Occasionally, my friends seemed to feel that they needed to help me with what ever I was doing. This was their perception speaking; I usually wanted to be self-sufficient and didn't ask for much help. After all, I had to be able to operate on my own, if possible - I have always felt this way. I seldom look to others for assistance just because I have only one hand. My methods may seem awkward to others, but they work well for me, and after a time, feel quite natural.

Now 35 years later, I have no recollection of ever having a right hand. Just my arm with a blunt stub on the end seems quite normal. I use my left hand to do things that require fingers to pick up and manipulate things. The right arm does a lot of steadying and holding. It even can open doors when my hand is full because I've replaced all door "knobs" with simple lever handles. These don't require twisting with a hand. There are few knobs on doors in Europe, but mostly they have handles. It's sad that this never caught on here in America.

The reunion with my grandma and grandpa was a teary-eyed experience. It was the first real cry I had since the accident. It was comforting to be reminded that my parents and grandparents really cared about me. These feelings are probably taken for granted. It often takes time to come to this realization. They felt better when they learned that I had been back to work and that I didn't expect this to have any affect on my job.

How people close to me would take my "accident" didn't occur to me. I think I'm often a bit over confident. If it doesn't bother me, I feel it won't bother other people. This, of course, isn't always the way things work. There were some things that I thought I wouldn't ever be able to do again, but I soon found out I was wrong.

When I was in my hospital bed thinking about my activities at work, I didn't think I'd ever be able to use my twin-lens reflex camera again. It was a complicated camera, which I used for most of the black-and-white photography. I had just started taking pictures for the new school catalog the week before the accident. I had a deadline to meet and had to continue, as I was "the" school photographer.

When I returned to work Thursday, I had to continue taking pictures, or I'd never get all the departments shot in time. The camera had knobs, levers and adjustments on all sides of it. It was difficult to operate, even with two hands, I expected this to be quite a challenge!

First, I had to load the film. Tension had to be maintained on the film roll as it was loaded, to prevent its unrolling. I couldn't begin to explain this tricky process, but to my surprise, I was able to do it! I had to consider every move of my remaining five fingers. I would hold one part, while opening or prying others. The fact that I was always left-handed helped, I'm sure. After the camera was loaded, I had to figure a way to hold the camera, focus it, then release the shutter - all with one hand, and while holding the camera steady. Most of my pictures were shot without a flash. This necessitated the use of a very slow shutter. The slightest movement of the camera meant out-of-focus pictures. Considering all of the things I did with one hand, operating this camera had to be the most difficult. It didn't take me long to get the hang of it, (I had no other choice if I was to be gainfully employed).

Today the world of right-handed camera controls hasn't changed much. At least I don't have to bother loading film in my present camera. But the location of the shutter release definitely is laid out for a right hand operation. I have to grip the camera in the crotch between my thumb and index finger. Then I reach around with my second finger to press the shutter release. If I want to zoom in, I have to grab the lens and turn it, then go back to the "shutter grip." This wouldn't work well if I was doing a lot of action shots.

Processing the film was my next challenge. It had to be loaded onto a processing reel in total darkness, by feel. Only after the film was all wound onto the reel and placed into the developing tank with the cover screwed on, could the lights be turned on.

My right arm could not be used at all, as its end was wrapped up in a large bandage. I really felt helpless. After healing, my right arm with out a hand on it became very useful. I think I'd feel handicapped if I didn't have my shorter right arm. Soon, however, I found that if I pressed the reel against something on the counter top, it would stay in place while I inserted the end of the film into the slots. Once I got the film into the grooves of the reel, I could ratchet the two halves of it with my thumb and forefinger, while steadying the opposite side with my fingers. Keep in mind, I couldn't see what I was doing, it all was by feel. It took me longer to process the film, but after a few rolls, I was soon doing it in the normal amount of time.

Hanging up the wet roll of film was impossible upon my first attempt. I had to open the film hanger clip, while inserting the end of the long roll of film. Normally, the film is held in one hand, while the other squeezes open the film hanger. I discovered that I could hold the end of the wet roll of film with my teeth, while opening the film hanger with my hand. It worked just fine!

Challenge after challenge was met and overcome in the darkroom, with one hand - and in the dark! My new methods seemed quite awkward at first, but soon, I didn't give them a second thought. I began to realize how a hook at the end of my arm could be very useful. I was becoming anxious to get my new prosthesis.

Before the "accident," I bought a new chainsaw. I had used it once, out on Pete's farm. Now with only one hand, I couldn't use it at all! I went out with Pete one weekend to cut wood. They used my saw while I looked on enviously. I began to seek some way to join in the fun. The ball of bandages at the end of my arm was inhibiting. What a joy to just have a useful stub to work with!

At home the next night, I decided that I had to devise some sort of temporary prosthesis so that I could use my own saw. I couldn't be fitted with a permanent prosthesis until my arm had completely healed and the swelling had subsided. This could be weeks away. I looked around the house for some ideas. I noticed my malted milk mixer in the kitchen, and the stainless steel container that the malt is made in. I slipped the container over the end of my right arm. It fit perfectly! It was just the right size to allow the bandaged end of my arm to fit inside. What a find!

On the way home from work the next day, I bought a clothes line hook. I drilled a hole in the end of the container and bolted the hook through the hole, with the nut on the inside. It looked very much like a pirate's hook, except that it wasn't sharp on the end. I had to then figure out how to make it stay on the end of my arm so that I could lift with it.

I knew Pete's arm held the secret, but he always wore a long-sleeved shirt. He felt embarrassed about showing his prosthesis. He could get by with allowing only the hook at the end to be seen sticking out of his shirt sleeve. I couldn't easily tell how his arm was held onto him. The next day when he came over, I eagerly showed him my new arm and explained that I didn't know how to make it stay on. I could sense that he wasn't eager to divulge this information. It had always been difficult for him to talk about himself. He felt very uncomfortable talking about something so personal as how his prosthesis was held on.

Ever so carefully, I pried into his secret.

"I have the arm part figured out," I said to him as we stood at my work bench, "But I have to somehow make it stay on my arm so I can lift. How does yours stay there?"

"It has straps that hold it," he said reluctantly, not wanting to get into a long conversation about it.

"Where are they connected to the plastic shell?" I asked, pressing on.

"Well, at the top end," he said, as he felt the upper end of his prosthesis through his shirt with his hand.

"I know, but are there one or two straps?"

"Well, there's one that goes up over my shoulder," he said motioning with his hand, "and across my back."

I was getting only as much information as I could pry out of him, but at least I was getting somewhere, so I continued.

"Maybe you could draw a diagram of how it's arranged... Here, use this pad."

He drew a simple diagram as best he could. He had to learn to write with his left hand after his accident, and his drawing wasn't very clear, but I got the general idea. It was almost like gaining possession of a secret treasure map!

"That's going to look pretty funny, just like Captain Hook!" he said playfully.

"I guess so," I replied, "but at least I won't have to stand around and watch you guys work all day!"

"Yeah, now you know how I felt before I had my arm," he said beaming.

I felt a glow inside. It was good to be able to shift some of Pete's emotional pain back to me for a change. I didn't mind at all. I could feel the radiation of his new superior position. It had been a long hard struggle for him. I allowed him every possible opportunity to feel important.

"They really do a good job over at Wisconsin Orthopedic," I said, looking at his prosthesis. "Your arm is a work of art, compared to my contraption!"

"But it's really ingenious how you put it together!" he said.

I was always amazed at how he would open up and talk more easily about personal matters after he received compliments and positive reinforcement. These were such beautifully clear examples during our interpersonal relationships.

Soon I began to construct a harness using some old leather belts which I bolted onto the steel container. It was crude, but it did keep my new prosthesis from falling off my arm!

The next weekend we went to the farm. I was proudly wearing my new arm, complete with a real hook. I was able to hold the chain saw with it, while operating the throttle and oiler button with my left hand. I wasn't able to work as hard as I wanted to because my arm was still tender. If I got to frisky with my hook, it would become painful. It was also winter, and because the prosthesis was made of steel, it had no insulating qualities. I had to go into the house to warm up quite often. At least I felt a bit more equal to the others, and was able to be somewhat productive. It also felt good to be able to let Pete feel superior for a change with his professionally made prosthesis.

Being the type of person that I am, I'm always looking for a better way. It wasn't long before I wanted to be able to do more with my hook. I went to Wisconsin Orthopedic where I had been several times with Pete, and purchased a "Farmers" type of hook or "Work Hook" as it's some times referred to. This was the same kind of terminal device that Pete had. It was specially developed for farmers and other working people. It was made of stainless steel and very durable. I had a nut welded on to the end of my malt container in the shop at school, so I could easily screw the hook into the end of the container/arm. This added an additional problem to my project, however. This new hook could be opened, a tremendously useful feature. It would enable me to grasp and hold objects with the hook. The problem was how to make it open. So it was back to Pete and his secret harness system.

Pete was reluctant to take his shirt off so I could see exactly how his hook was rigged. He finally consented to draw a diagram on paper, which was a bit difficult to follow, but I managed.

I had my mother sew some straps out of a heavy canvas material. I used a spare clutch cable from my Honda bike which I connected to the straps. This went over my right shoulder and under my left armpit. The end of the cable was connected to the hook, and pulled it open when tension was applied by moving my right arm and shoulder. It was a hassle to get everything positioned correctly so that the hook would open with the least amount of effort. These were the details that I wasn't able to get from Pete. It would have been a lot easier if he could have been a live model for me. Interestingly I can recall several years later seeing Pete sitting around at home with out his shirt on. His self-confidence and self-worth feelings had greatly improved. He wasn't the shy amputee that he was when I first met him. This made me feel really good.

I used my home-made prosthesis at work. I was getting tired of waiting for the swelling to go down so I could be fitted with a real arm. It seemed to be taking a long time.

Ray, the prosthetist who was going to make my arm, checked my progress weekly. After the second week, he said that the stump of my arm wasn't shrinking as it was supposed to. It seems that I needed to keep the end of my arm wrapped tightly with a stretch bandage, twenty-four hours a day. I had been taking the bandage off during the day when I wore my home-made arm, thus the swelling wasn't going down. This wasn't made clear to me at the hospital, or at subsequent visits to the doctor's office for checkups. Thus my shrinking was going far slower than it should have.

After I began to wrap the end of my arm every day, the swelling began to subside. I avoided wrapping my arm because it was so difficult to do with one hand. Ray called me "skinny minnie", as we began to notice a decrease in the size of my stump. If he had fitted me with a prosthesis while my arm was enlarged, it would have been much too loose when it shrunk down to normal size. Ray had a very keen sense of awareness in dealing with his patients. Ray himself lost his leg as a teen. He fully understood that losing a limb could be a very traumatic experience. His sensitivity enabled him to relate to his clients appropriately.

After waiting several more weeks, Ray finally announced, after measuring my stump, that we could make an appointment for him to begin to fit my "real" arm. I could hardly contain myself.

At the time, Pete had the advantage over me. He had the use of his hook. At times he was helping me out. I'll never forget the night we went down to the newsstand to buy a tin of our favorite pipe tobacco. It came in a flat, round can, which was vacuum sealed and had a screw-off lid. I had developed a great dislike for tight lids.

We decided to fill our pipes before returning home. We soon discovered that we couldn't get the top off. Pete with one hand and a hook, me with only one hand; what a pair!

We got out of the car and put the can down on the pavement in the middle of the street. Fortunately, it was late at night and there was little traffic. Pete held the can between his feet while we attempted to twist the lid off. We grunted, strained, swore and broke fingernails. The cover wouldn't budge. Neither of us could get enough of a grip on it to twist it off.

Finally, in desperation, we returned to the store to ask the man behind the counter if he would open the can for us. As it was dark outside, we couldn't read the large letters around the edge of the can that read, "TO OPEN, INSERT COIN AND TWIST." The clerk put a penny under the edge of the lid and popped it open instantly!

CHAPTER 5

My New Arm

I had hoped to get my new arm by my birthday. March thirty-first came and went. It took longer than I anticipated to go through the process of being fitted for my new prothesis. I was very eager to get it and carry on with my life. This enthusiastic attitude isn't shared by all amputees, however. It took Pete a long time to accept his situation, and to decide to begin to wear his new arm.

Perhaps we should consider if a prosthesis should even be used. Although I was an enthusiastic prosthetic user in the beginning, I do not feel that it is essential that one always be used. Over the years I've encountered many stories about amputees who were once again able to carry on with their lives because they were fitted with some new prosthetic device. Often these stories tell how these persons lives were torn and shattered by their disability, before being fitted with the new limb. I am often amused by the enthusiasm of the writer who was obviously impressed by the device and did not have an understanding of how the users' attitude is more likely to determine the individuals' success, than the device itself.

As useful as an arm prosthesis can be, it isn't as vital to the wearer as a leg prosthesis however. We do have a choice in this instance. This choice is usually based on function and appearance. A construction worker would depend heavily on a steel hook; a public figure would be understandably more interested in a natural looking hand. Despite my own eagerness however, I must admit that I don't feel that a prosthesis should be considered mandatory for every dismembered person at all times--there are many factors to be considered.

We've already seen how difficult it can be for some to accept such a device emotionally. Now let's consider the purely physical and mechanical aspects of this decision.

The foremost consideration that comes to mind is the type of work and leisure-time activities the person is engaged in. The second may be the individuals' comfort.

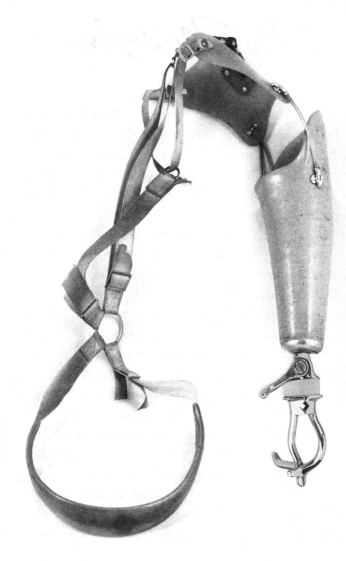

Let's begin with the vocational considerations; I am what I call a "do-er". I am an active person, always building, changing, fixing and trying something new. There are some things that are just about impossible to do without a prosthesis and sometimes even a specialized terminal device, other than a "conventional" hook. Though I probably could, I would not want to ride a motorcycle one-handed. I did once; I went down the street about four blocks away, to get a cup of coffee for a friend at a gas station. In order not to spill it, I held the rather soft paper cup with my hook, while operating the bike with my left hand. It worked, but I wouldn't want to do it often, or in front of a policeman. I doubt he'd approve. Ones' balance control is rather marginal.

Typing does not work well using only one hand. I've seen some very good water skiers that had only one arm, but it was a very strong arm. I find it much easier to use both arms. Although many people snow ski with one pole, I prefer two. Although I can ride my ten-speed bike without my prosthesis, and usually do in the heat of the summer, I prefer the stability of using two arms. It is rather difficult to row a boat in a straight line with one arm, or paddle a canoe single handedly--we don't have much choice here. I find it almost impossible to lift and carry some of the heavy electronics equipment and boxes that I use in my work without my prosthesis. I would have to resort to other methods, such as hand trucks and carts, and still may need help to get them onto the cart. Operating farm machinery isn't impossible with one hand, but a prosthesis does make it easier, because often two operations must be accomplished at the same time with two controls. Shoveling and raking is much easier and more efficient with a prosthesis. These are but a few specific tasks that benefit from the use of two hands. Aside from these specifics, the choice of using a prosthesis or not, is mostly a choice based on personal preference rather than on necessity. Also self-image can play a critical part in this decision. How much does it bother you to have one empty sleeve? I doubt that you'd ever hear this from a prosthetic salesman, fitter or even a doctor. This kind of information comes from many years of personal experience.

Function is very important when considering if we should use a prosthesis. If I were going to employ a leaf and grass raker for instance, it wouldn't take me long to realize that two hands work better than one. I would choose a two-handed person over the one-hander because of speed and efficiency. Add a prosthesis to the picture and the situation becomes just about equal among workers. Incidentally, I would suggest that job applicants wear their prosthesis when applying. If nothing else, the employer will have the impression that the applicant appears about equal to others, or at least has a fighting chance. Also, many job situations simply do not require two strong hands.

Personal comfort is another consideration. In the summer when the temperature is in the eighties and very humid, I don't wear my arm at all. I wouldn't have a coat sleeve to fill out for aesthetic reasons. I am much more comfortable without my prosthesis. At work, I am able to perform my television production job with one hand (typing excepted).

Let's take a closer look at the body-powered prosthesis, in order to understand why it can be uncomfortable. The shell of the arm is made of fiberglass cloth and resin. The end of the arm that wears this shell is covered by a wool sock for cushioning and perspiration absorption. It can become very hot inside the shell in the summer, as well as very cold in the winter. This shell is suspended onto the body of the wearer by a harness made of nylon straps. These straps can be uncomfortable when it's hot if they are directly against the body, without the cushioning afforded by a tee skirt. However, a tee shirt worn under a dress shirt can be quite a hot combination. Thus, we see that a tee shirt is needed for comfort because of the straps, but it is also quite hot when wearing two shirts in the summer. I am assuming most people would prefer to wear a shirt over the straps when in public for aesthetic reasons.

It is interesting to note here that being fat has an advantage in this situation: Fat is a wonderful body pad which makes the harness assembly more comfortable to wear. I was about twenty pounds heavier when I was fitted with my first arm, than I am at present. I found that the straps against my body didn't bother me compared to now, without the extra fat cushion. This is especially true with leg wearers. They need as much cushioning as possible because of the body weight which presses down on the end of the stump inside the prosthetic leg.

Let me give you a first-hand, (or should I say one hand) comfort-based choice of use. The first summer I had my prosthesis, I sold my house in the city and bought a farm. It was unimproved, so I had to install plumbing, electricity and a heating system. I probably wore my arm only fifty percent of the time, because of the summer heat.

Accomplishing these tasks wasn't unusually difficult without the use of my prosthesis. There were times when it may have been inconvenient, but the house did get finished. I was able to do the work necessary with one hand and the stump of one arm. My prosthesis often hung on a nail on the back porch.

I find it interesting to note that I am more concerned about being comfortable now, than ten years ago when I was first fitted. In the beginning, I was quite anxious to have something that would replace my lost hand, no matter what the cost or inconvenience. Also, I think people in their teens are more tolerant than people over forty. Now that the "newness" of it has worn off, my prosthesis isn't as important to me as it was in the beginning. I think most newly amputated persons would have difficulty understanding this. Pete once told me that his prosthesis was his most important possession. At that time in his life, I'm sure this was quite true.

At last I could be fitted with my new arm. The swelling has subsided and Ray was about to make a "real" arm for me. although my make-shift home made device had served me well, I knew it was a far cry from the professionally crafted arm that I was about to receive. As a child, I have memories of thinking that these hooks mush have been somehow screwed right into the end of the persons arm. Now the secret process was about to be revealed to me at last.

The fitting began with a stockinette that Ray pulled over the end of my amputated arm. It was held up by temporary straps and clips that he attached to my shirt. He wrapped a water-soaked plaster bandage around the stockinette, building up several layers. Ray then carefully molded the shape of this cast with his hands as it hardened, in order to duplicate the normal contour of the end of my arm. In the case of an arm that is off just below the elbow, the cast is made with the elbow flexed to ninety degrees. This is because he must also consider the elbow in his manufacture, when a forearm is very short.

Perhaps a word about body weight is in order here; if a person weighs 200 pounds at the time of being cast for an arm, and then later loses weight, the person's limb will shrink considerably. A prosthesis that was the correct size at the time of the original fitting will now be too large. The person's arm will rattle around inside of it. This is the voice of experience speaking... Extra resin can be added to the inside, or a soft foam insert can be made to take up the extra space, but you may look a bit strange with one fat and one thin arm! The terminal device (hook) and body straps can be transferred to a newly made properly fitting arm, thereby saving you about $300 over the cost of a complete arm.

Of course, the reverse situation can also occur; suppose you had been successfully fitted with a new arm, but it took you a long time to overcome your depression, and you found you could make yourself feel much better by constantly eating everything in sight. One morning, while dressing to go to your weekly depression support group, you discovered your arm simply couldn't be jammed into your prosthesis anymore, even with a thinner arm sock! Now you're in trouble and have two possible solutions; you can be fitted for a new arm, (less the cost of a new hook, which can be transferred to the new prosthesis) or join Weight Watchers and gradually shrink back into it again.

Back in Ray's fitting room, the plaster bandage on my arm had hardened. It was easily removed because of the stockinette inside, against my skin. A solid plaster mould of my stump was then made by filling the wrapped cast with plaster and inserting a holding rod into the soft plaster. Ray then shaped this mould with a rasp so that the final shell would represent my arm in exactly the right shape.

Next, Ray made what he called a "check socket" from this master mould. It was made of bees wax and stockinette. Several layers of molten wax and netting were used. Because the wax is easy to work with, Ray was able to carefully cut, trim and adjust the shape and fit of this check socket until he was satisfied that it fit properly. He was also able to identify points of pressure and bend the wax or even add layers until it fit me like a glove.

Once he was satisfied with the fit of the bees wax check socket, he poured a lamination mould. This was a corrected plaster reproduction of my arm. With this final step, he was ready to make an arm.

The plaster was covered with layers of polyester resin and nylon stockinette. The inner wall conformed to the exact shape of my arm, the outer wall was built up to the finished arm shape, and also incorporated the wrist unit. This device provided the threaded socket for the attachment of the terminal device.

I had a choice of several types of wrists. Pete's was a friction type. His hook was screwed into the wrist unit until it encountered a metal washer and rubber compression ring. By turning his hook further in, the rubber ring became compressed, allowing the hook to rotate, but with a bit of resistance. the position of the hook was thus continually adjustable, to suit his needs. The hook position was maintained by the compression of the rubber ring.

There was also the choice of either a round or oval wrist shape. I chose the oval shape, as I felt it looked more natural. I chose a wrist unit that used an allen-head screw, which tightened against a nylon bushing to hold the position of my terminal device. I wanted to be able to tighten or loosen the hook when I wanted to ride my cycle, and operate the throttle with my hook. Ten years later, when I had another arm made, I chose the compression ring wrist. I now had to remove the control cable from the hook, and turn it several times in order to relieve the pressure on the compression ring, allowing the hook to turn freely. This proved to be an easy task. I found that I did have to replace the nylon insert in the first wrist unit several times a year, because it would wear out. With this wrist, I am still on my first compression ring. It seems there is nothing to wear out.

Also available are wrist units with "click" stop positions, and quick-change units that allow various terminal devices to be inserted and removed easily. A special flexation wrist allows the hook to be flexed in three positions, just as one flexes a hand at the end of the wrist. This extra flexation feature is especially useful to those who are missing both hands. It allows them the advantage of positioning the hook to reach body areas that a ridged hook could not.

I had already purchased a hook to use with my home made prosthesis. It was a Dorrance number 07, or "farmers' hook". This is what Pete had, it seemed to be quite versatile and was made of stainless steel. All of these hooks are split down the middle, and open to allow the user to grasp or pinch objects, much the way one would with the thumb and forefingers.

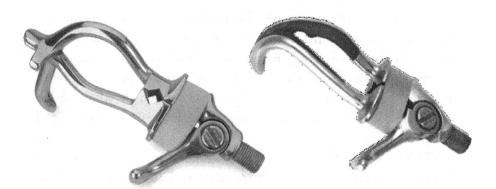

The "Farmers Hook" is on the left. The hook
with rubber on the inside is on the right.

An alternate type of hook is the Dorrance 555. The inside of the
pre-shaped fingers are neoprene rubber lined. I almost feel somewhat
handicapped when I use this style. It does not have the ability to grasp
objects and prevent them from slipping out of its' grip, compared to the
farmers' hook. I do favor the aluminum hook, however, for typing, and
keyboard work. It weighs about three ounces, compared to the much
heavier steel hook. Being very light, my arm response when typing is quite
quick. I find the steel hook "pounds" the keys with too much force, and
the weight slows me down. The aluminum hooks' inner rubber gripping
surface seems to work the best on a motorcycle throttle and hand-grip.
The rubber-to-rubber contact is much more positive than that found with
steel hooks. The simple, curved design will also slip off the handlebar of a
bike or cycle is one should fall down, a much safer situation. The farmers'
hook will not unless it is pulled open via the control cable. I have ridden
for several years with both types of hooks, and prefer the 555 style on my
bike. The aluminum hook is not durable, and is easily bent, so it should
not be used for heavy work. It does a poor job of gripping the handle of a
rake, shovel, or fork, so the handle slips out of the hook quite easily. The
farmers' hook, on the other hand, has a round opening designed especially
for this purpose, one of many little special features that are very useful
when doing manual labor.

The light aluminum hook is desirable for above-elbow amputees because they use a mechanical elbow with either an electrical or mechanical lift to raise their forearm. Generally, above elbow amputees are also less likely to do heavy work with this arm, and therefore do not always need the strength of the heavy steel hook. As is often the case, there are always exceptions. I personally know a farmer that does have a mechanical elbow, and uses a farmers' hook. He does have the problem of frequent damage to the elbow mechanism because of mechanical overloads.

A final possible terminal device, which became available in the early 1980's is called the Prehensile hand. It's shaped somewhat like a crab pincer. It is spring-loaded to stay open. It closes only when tension is applied to the control cable. I tried this "hand" and found the voluntary-closing design to be quite a hassle. The Dorrance hooks are closed by four to six heavy rubber bands, made especially for this purpose--they will always grip objects, the bands providing the closing power. The operation of the Prehensile Hand, however, requires a constant pull of the control cable to grasp objects. If this pull (provided by the strap under the opposite arm) is relaxed, the hand will drop what ever is being held. I found this very inconvenient. My armpit also became sore because I had to constantly use the strap which ran under it, in order to keep the hand closed when holding an object. The slightest loss of concentration or relaxation of tension would cause the object I was holding to crash to the floor. A ratchet locking device was provided which would lock the hand and allow carrying, but it was not strong, and the instructions said it could be broken easily.

In contrast, when I used my arm for the first time, with the farmers' hook attached, I was amazed at how easy and natural its' operation was. When I wanted to open it a small amount, I would extend my arm out slightly from my shoulder. The amount of closing tension was easily controllable by slight arm/shoulder movements. The best part was that I could relax this movement, and the hook would continue to grasp the object for carrying, with out fear of dropping it. This operation seemed to me to be quite natural, as compared to that of the Prehensile Hand. Also, I found it was almost impossible to type with it, because of its shape. All styles of hooks can be used to type. I did find that it worked quite well for riding my bicycle, however. It had a positive, firm grasp of the handle grip. The Prehensile Hand also lacked the "tweezers" type of pinch, or grip that hooks provide. This can be very useful for the very fine work that one often does with the fingernails of the thumb and forefingers. Although the device was well made and much engineering went into its design, I personally found it quite awkward, as compared to most hooks.

Life continued to be a challenge while Ray was building my arm. Buying an ice cream cone was a potentially frustrating and embarrassing situation. Most people take the cone with one hand and present the money with the other. With only one hand to work with, what does a pralines-n'-cream freak do? May I suggest this procedure... While the person behind the counter is scooping the ice cream, ask how much it will cost. If you have the correct change, no problem. Place the money on the counter and wait for the cone. Don't forget tax. If you don't have the correct change, hand over the bill while the person still has the cone. Then they have to deal with the situation. They make the change, and hand it to you. You pocket the change, then take the cone--a one-hand transaction. If the person attempts to hand the cone to you before the money transaction, ask them to "wait a moment please," while you dig into your pocket. As you leave, pray that the door does not have a twist type knob.

I was on pins and needles for two weeks while waiting for my new arm. At last a call came from Ray; I could come over that afternoon to try it on. I felt like I was somehow going to be a new person. Perhaps it was the prospect of being able to have my shirts and coats fit properly once again. Although I had known Pete for quite a while, much of what I had assumed about living with one hand and a hook was about to become reality for myself.

When Ray brought my finished arm into the fitting room, I'm sure I was grinning from ear-to-ear, it was beautiful! I had never shown him the arm I made, it couldn't begin to compare. His creation was even colored, what I called "prosthetic pink". It looked flesh colored. I slipped on one of the wool socks that Ray gave me, put my arm through the harness, and into the plastic shell. It really did fit like a glove! It felt so snug and secure, compared to my old malt-container arm. Ray took a few minutes to adjust the harness so that the pull on the control cable which opened the hook, was just right. Then it was ready to be tried. I extended my elbow slightly to my side, which pulled at the strap going under my opposite armpit. This movement caused the cable to pull the hook open. I couldn't believe how easily it opened. Ray used a teflon liner inside the cable housing, and a nylon covered cable. It pulled the hook open like butter. If the amputee has had skin burns in the area where the straps touch the skin, a layer of soft tee-shirt material is definitely needed to protect the tender skin from friction. Ray also said that my arm would feel best if I used a clean, dry sock each day. The special all-wool sock cushions the arm inside the shell.

Children as young as three to five years old can be fitted with prostheses. They may not always want to use the arm, but it does allow them to become accustomed to being able to use both arms during their important developing years.

I am sure that Ray derives a great deal of pleasure and satisfaction from seeing his clients "renewed" when they are fitted with a new prosthesis. I found it to be better than I had anticipated. I felt as though I was now ready to conquer the world, at long last.

CHAPTER 6

—————————

At Work & Play

When one begins to perform a task using the hands, the dominant (generally the right) hand is the one that does most of the delicate or "educated" work. The other hand usually does the menial job of holding and steadying for the "talented" hand. A non-functioning human hand could substitute for these lesser tasks of holding and steadying, even the stub of an amputated arm or one with a prosthetic device on its end could perform this task.

Let's take a look at what can be accomplished with one hand and a hook, and how the techniques might differ from those employed by two-handed people. The initial impression of most people who meet me for the first time is that my abilities are probably limited to some degree because of my hook. I often hear kind offers of, "Can I help you?" As a "one-hander" of over thirteen years, let me attempt to dispel this handicap myth.

Recently, I was sitting with a friend, making a list of everything we could think of that I thought would be impossible for a person with one hook to accomplish. We had difficulty finding things to put on this list. Every time she would think of something, I could explain how I did it, and that I didn't feel it was a difficult task. Here is my list:

Playing most musical instruments.

Using a hand operated can opener.

It would seem from the lack of items in the above list that losing a hand does not necessarily make much of a difference in one's ability. There is often a difference in technique, to some extent. There are also varying degrees of extremity loss. I am usually referring to my own condition, where the hand was severed about two inches above the wrist. Functionally, this is an ideal residual arm length; the forearm is long enough to afford good leverage with the prosthesis, yet is short enough to allow room for the mechanics of the wrist unit in the end of it. In situations where the forearm below the elbow is very short, or where the elbow is missing entirely, the function of the prosthetic arm is limited, depending on how much arm remains below the shoulder. Shoulder disarticulations present even further limitations. Two prosthetic arms will be dealt with in another chapter.

Let me begin with what cannot be done, as the list is quite short. Most musical instruments are designed to be played with ten fingers. Even the loss of part of one finger can present difficulty for the musician. A rock album was released around 1980, by a group who had their picture on the cover. Unfortunately, I cannot recall their name, but they had a bass guitarist who was missing a hand, and he played with a prosthesis/hook. I played bass with a neighborhood band the year before I lost my hand. About a year later, I longed to make music once again, and bought a used instrument. I found I was able to play reasonably well using a felt pick which I held with my hook, rather than my fingers as I had before. The hook did not have the agility of my lost fingers, but I did make music. I could also play by "hammering down", or striking the strings against the frets rather than simply pressing them down with the fingers of my left hand. An auto harp could also be played with a pick held by a hook. The hook could conceivably hold a bow to play other string instruments, but the agility of the wrist and fingers adds greatly to one's playing ability.

Let's discuss in detail a variety of tasks, both work and play, and some techniques that can be used to accomplish them.

For fun, let's try tennis. I have found my prosthesis does not really assist me in playing the game. It might possibly be used for serving the ball, but I find I cannot open the hook with the proper timing to release the ball. I play without my arm, for maximum comfort, and serve the ball by tossing it up with the same hand that holds the racket. My fingers grip both the racket handle and the ball, while I toss. I am quite pleased with this technique. Much more so than I am with the game that usually follows.

Paddling a canoe with a hand and hook works very well. Here, again, I recommend a farmer's hook because of its special design for holding objects with handles. Paddling works slightly better on my right side, because the paddle is "steered" or turned and controlled from the top end, where the hand grips the paddle. A hook cannot perform this turning function. When switching to the left side, I still turn the paddle with my hand, but this time from the middle of the paddle, rather than from the top, as would usually be the case. Unfortunately the prosthesis does not prevent one's arms and shoulders from becoming any less tired.

I have never played golf. It would seem, however, that a bit of sponge rubber, like that used on racing bike handle grips, could be used to tighten up the grip of the hook on a club. A bit of experimentation here should take care of any problems caused by the metal of the hook against the metal of the club.

The diameter of a baseball bat is just about right to fit the opening in the Dorrance 07 farmer's hook. The bat is swung in the normal manner. Catching is mostly one-handed.

After I lost my hand, and before I was fitted with my prosthesis, I sold my Honda 500cc motorcycle. Not because I thought that I could never ride it again, but because they came out with a new 350cc bike which had all the advantages of the four cylinders, yet was much lighter and easier to handle. I never liked the weight of the 500. The new bike arrived before my arm, and I had to be content to watch my friends try it out. At last my arm was finished and I could ride my shiny new bike. I found that the grip of my prosthesis on the right handle bar felt real strange. Strange, because my hook didn't give me the usual feeling of gripping the handlebar that I was accustomed to. The sensation of grip on the throttle was totally missing; how much I was turning it and how hard I was holding on. My hook's grip was secure enough, but because the sense of feeling was missing, I didn't fully trust it at first. I operated the throttle by loosening the hook, so that it would swivel freely in the wrist socket. Rotation of the throttle was accomplished by moving my arm in and out from the side of my body, which would, in turn, rotate the throttle grip. But because of the lack of feeling, I had to train my brain to trust what it could not feel, and believe that my new arm and hook could indeed hang on and balance me when I let go of the left grip with my hand. After a while, I could comfortably turn the bike while holding on with only my hook. It took many weeks of riding to accept this new feeling.

I was using the 07 farmer's hook. The opening was too large (this is the larger of the two hooks available) to grip the standard, factory-supplied solid rubber handgrip. In order to gain enough friction to actually turn the throttle, I had to press my arm outward, causing it to bind in the opening of the hook, and thereby rotate when I moved my arm. I rode several months using this technique before I decided there must be a better way. I found out from Ray that there was an aluminum hook available, the Dorrance 5XA with neoprene rubber on the inside gripping surface. I got one of these, and changed the standard hard-rubber grips on the bike to balloon-like soft grips. This resulted in a very effective rubber-to-rubber grip that was really super! I no longer had to exert outward pressure with my arm to turn the throttle. I also took the return spring off the throttle linkage, which made pulling open the four carburetors even easier. This also meant that I had to turn the throttle closed when I wanted to slow down. It would no longer return by itself if let go. This might seem to be an unsafe condition, but in actuality, I have never had any problems. I could now cruise for hours without getting tired. In fact, one summer I rode from Northern Wisconsin to Tennessee with a friend on our bikes and found the whole arrangement very comfortable. His throttle hand would get tired after a while, but I never felt a thing!

Because the front brake on my bike was operated by a hand lever on the right side next to the throttle grip, I was unable to us it because my hook could not squeeze it as with a hand. I rode for about 2 years using the foot brake, which operated only the rear drum. The disadvantage in this situation was that if I needed to make a quick, hard stop, the rear wheel would lock up and slide. My stopping ability was reduced. One day I discovered a device in a Chicago automotive parts and accessory catalog that would operate the front hydraulic brake at the same time the rear brake pedal was pressed. This could greatly increase my stopping ability and would be much safer. I ordered the unit and installed it. It worked perfectly. This was the final and crowning touch to my motorcycling refinements.

My first time on water skis after I lost my hand was quite an adventure. It seemed that all I had to do was "hook" onto the tow rope handle and go. I was right, I popped out of the water, dropped a ski and was off. I ran into difficulty, however, when I leaned too far over and lost it. My left hand let go of the handle, but my hook didn't understand what was happening and continued to hang on for dear life. In a flash, my prosthesis was torn from my body by the powerful ski boat. When I came to the surface and realized what had happened, I glanced at the water around me to see if my arm was anywhere near. I spotted it a short distance away bobbing up and down. I swam over to it quickly and discovered that it didn't sink to the bottom of the lake because the inside of the arm socket didn't fill with water. What a relief! I doubt that I would have found it if it had. It was very clear to me that I needed to devise a new method of hanging onto the ski rope. No one ever told me I couldn't do these things because I lost a hand, so I often had to discover a new way the hard way!

I worked with an instructor in the welding shop at school and designed a terminal device that would prevent my weekend adventure from reoccurring. We took a three inch length of stainless steel pipe about one and a half inches in diameter and cut it in half length wise. I took my original number seven farmer's hook, which had a larger opening than the one I usually used, and cut the "fingers" off of it, leaving the part that screwed into my arm and the hinge portion with two stubs on it where the hook used to be. We welded the two halves of the pipe on to the stubs. I now had a terminal device that opened like a clamshell instead of a hook. With this new device, I was able to grip the handle of the tow rope very tightly, (depending upon the number of rubber bands which held it closed) yet it would open automatically if I fell. The control cable opened the grip as my arm extended from me while falling, thus releasing the rope. Even if this naturally occurring action didn't take place, a strong pull on the rope was enough to yank the rope out of its grip. I didn't do any more standing starts because the jerk would snatch the rope out of my device - a small price to pay to be able to ski again.

In Wisconsin, the water soon freezes over again and we put on narrower skis and lost of warm clothes. We call this sport down hill skiing. However, before the hills opened, I had yet another problem to solve. Pete had been skiing holding his ski pole with his number six farmer's hook. Because the actual amount of gripping surface was small, the pole swung rather uncontrollably from the end of his arm. He wasn't able to plant it exactly where he wanted to.

I decided to use a mechanical hand to hold the pole in the usual manner. It had spring-loaded fingers that were normally closed in a gripping position. The hand was quite strong, but heavy. The mechanism was covered with a skin-like, natural looking rubber glove. It even had veins, fingernails and hair. I fine tuned its grasp by cutting and filing a groove into the rubber hand grip on the pole, to allow the fingers to seat better around the handle. I found that even the thin, single layer of a leather glove caused the grip to become loose and a bit sloppy, causing me to lose the pole often when skiing hard. Without the glove, the grip was more positive and secure, allowing me to forget what the right hand was doing and concentrate on my skiing. This "naked" hand may have looked a bit strange in below freezing weather, but I was more concerned about its function than its looks. I think I had given up looking the part of a good skier many years ago in favor of ability and technique.

In spring, some men's fancies turn to bicycles. My attention turned to the improvement of the operation of the bike's gear shift levers. As it comes from the factory, the upper and lower shifters are usually mounted on the frame, close to the handlebars. This meant that I had to move my left hand from the handle bar to reach the shift levers. Shifting with my hook didn't work all that well. I didn't want to have to look down at the shifters, I preferred to keep my eyes ahead. My brother John suggested a shift mechanism that mounts inside the end of the handlebar, with the lever sticking out the end. This can be operated easily by the fingers without interrupting the grip on the handlebar. I decided that I didn't use the second - the high/low lever very often, so I left it mounted down on the frame.

As spring turns into summer, and the temperature goes up, I find that I often want to ride my bike when I am not wearing my arm. At first this seemed very unstable. Anything other than riding straight ahead made me feel like I was going to crash. My confidence improved after about two weeks of riding, and I soon felt quite comfortable. I also had to turn my handle bars upside-down, so that I could ride in an upright position. The usual riding position of leaning over the bars does not work well unless you can support your upper body with two arms. Thus, without the use of my prosthesis, I found that I had to sit upright while riding. As with my motorcycle, I again had the problem of hand controls for front and rear brakes. I purchased a hand control that was designed for a tandem bike, and would pull the front and rear brake cables at the same time. This solved my problem quite easily.

It was not the fact that I was riding my bicycle with one hand that almost did me in. It was the train tracks. I was on my way back to work from lunch one day when I decided to take a new route. A junction of two sets of tracks crossed the road in front of me. I swerved the left so that by the time I reached them, I could turn right and steer almost straight across the tracks to avoid getting my front wheel caught in between them. I was evidently going faster than I estimated, because I was upon the tracks before I had a chance to turn into them. The tracks grabbed my front wheel and down I went. I wasn't too badly banged up, I managed to break my fall with my left hand, so I limped on to work. That afternoon, my wrist began to ache. I thought I had sprained it. This was Wednesday. The pain persisted through the rest of the week. I made arrangements to help a friend build a deck at his summer home on the weekend. We were working with 2 X 10 lumber twelve feet long, and I was cutting them with a skill saw. I was disappointed that my wrist wasn't improving. When it still hurt Monday morning, I made an appointment to have the orthopedic specialist, who was the attending physician when I lost my hand, look at my wrist. The x-ray showed that I had fractured it, but he said that since it happened almost a week before, there was no point in putting a cast on it. I was glad to hear that as it was the only hand I had. Although it was sore and quite weak, I still had some use of it.

I'm getting hungry, let's eat. Opening a can of beans can be quite a challenge or even totally impossible. It depends on your disposition. I have always used a hand-operated can opener that had thick yellow plastic handles. Well, I don't anymore. I haven't found a way to make it work with a hand and one hook. I now use an electric opener. When you're hungry, there's nothing better than the smell of fresh-baked bread, just out of the oven. Cutting it with one hand and a hook is tricky. The hook cannot do a good job of holding the loaf without making holes in it. I solved this by taking my favorite bread knife out to my shop to modify the handle. I filed and ground the bone handle so that it could be grasped firmly by my farmer's hook. Now I "saw" the bread with the knife held by my hook, and my hand does the delicate job of holding the tender loaf steady. My hook does a good job of steadying the piece of bread for buttering. You need to spread toward the hook. Peanut butter is tricky, just be sure to always spread towards what ever is keeping the bread in place. This could even be a corner made of small strips of wood nailed to the bread board, which are about half the thickness of the average piece of bread. This is especially for spreading work. I use this same modified knife for most other cutting jobs, as it leaves my left hand free to grasp what ever I am working on in the kitchen. At the table, I am always amused by the fork/knife-switching tricks that Americans use while eating. I could never understand why the utensils couldn't be kept in the same hand and just used. I always hold the fork in my hand, and often cut with it too. For heavy-duty meats, I used to steady the piece with my hook and saw away with the knife in my hand. Lately I've dispensed with heavy cuts of red meat, so I don't have this problem anymore. Most of my eating is done with only my hand.

At social events, I often hold a bottle or glass with my hook so that I can use my hand to snack with. Most people eat corn-on-the-cob with a hand holding each end. I simply grab one end and eat. The little yellow handles that can be stuck into the ends of the cob also work well, with the square notch in my farmer's hook holding on end.

When mixing heavy dough like chocolate chip cookie dough, I prefer to use a very heavy, large crockery bowl. I often set it on the floor between my feet when it needs help to stay in place. Taking the cookies out of the oven is a snap. The all-steel hook can grasp the hot pans without getting burnt fingers. It can also do things like lift the lids on top of the cook stove to stuff in more wood, or grab a burning log that rolls out of the fireplace.

After eating, I usually use a sponge to do dishes. I fold it in half and grasp it with my hook. When I am not wearing my prosthesis, I just use the stub of my arm, shoving it down into glasses instead of tying to steady the glass in order to get a sponge into it with my hand. I steady the dishes in the sink with the end of my arm while wiping them with the sponge. I also prefer the single-handle type of mixing faucet. This can be operated by a hook or the end of an arm, as compared to individual hot and cold faucets which work best with a hand on each while adjusting the flow.

If you enjoy making pottery and other objects with clay, you would probably find it works well with a hand and the end of your arm. You can use the arm stub to form the clay much as you would use the palm of a hand.

I wear contact lenses. Handling, removing and inserting them poses no problem, but my techniques are probably a bit different. When cleaning them, I gently rub the lens between two fingers. Most people probably put the lens in the palm of a hand and rub it with a finger from the other hand. Insertion can be accomplished in any of three ways:

1. use the end of your hook to hod the upper eyelid up
2. use the end of your amputated arm if it is long enough
3. use your index finger, with the lens perched on the middle finger.

This last technique takes a bit of practice, but works fine.

A nurse friend told me of a surgeon who has an arm prosthesis. His hook goes into the autoclave with the rest of the surgical instruments for sterilization before the operation.

When I went back to work after my accident, I didn't think I would ever type again. I couldn't have been more wrong! Not only do I type as fast as I used to, but more than ever. As I mentioned before, the light aluminum hook works best. I use my hook just as one would use an index finger to type. I am able to type at perhaps 50 WPM. I like to have a rubber cushion on the end of my hook, to protect the switch contacts under the keys of the keyboard I am using. I use a computer, electronic typewriter and character generator for TV titling. I think, in time, all of these keyboards would be damaged by the pounding of a metal hook. A cap-type pencil eraser that is worn down can be slipped over the end of a hook. I have also smeared liquid silicone rubber over the end of my hook and shaped it before it hardened. I find that if it is much more than about an eighth of an inch thick, it causes "key bounce". This is when the hook actually bounces when it hits the key and causes two characters to appear. I have to glance down to see where the hook is hitting, but once I know that I am over the key, I find I can glance up again and continue typing. Everything on the right side of the keyboard is covered by my hook. My left hand covers the left side of the board and my thumb hits the space bar. When I occasionally use a manual typewriter, I find I almost pound with my hook, in order to make a dark impression. I certainly wouldn't suggest this technique with any electronic devices.

When I wash the car, I use the hook to grasp one end of the chamois cloth to wring it out. When not wearing my arm I fold the cloth over several times and put one end of it on the fence along side the car to hold it down with my arm while twisting it with my hand. I usually hold the hose with my hook while washing with my rag in hand.

My current car is an automatic, but I have been driving mostly manually shifted cars. I usually shift by pushing or pulling the floor lever with my farmer's hook just below the shift knob. The knob itself is usually of little use to the hook. I also find that a short length of rubber surgical tubing slipped over the shaft of the lever prevents a metal-to-metal clash when I shift. The number 5 hook does not work well here because it's curved shape allows it to slip off the shift lever when pushing it forward. The farmer's hook, with it's tab on the end does not have this problem. I can shift in the dark with it, but not with the 5XA.

Most states will require an amputee to be re-tested on the road when the license is up for renewal. If the vehicle used in the test is an automatic, the examiner will assume that the driver cannot shift a manual transmission. If the car is equipped with power steering, he will also assume that you cannot turn a car without it. Thus, in order to obtain a license without these restrictions, it is necessary to be tested in an all-manual vehicle. With the many small cars in use today, these assists are not as necessary as in the days of full-sized cars. I had a hassle when I was going to obtain a license to drive a semi truck in Idaho. There are many restrictions involved in this type of license. For various reasons I finally gave up. It all depends on where you intend to drive and how much effort you want to invest in obtaining the license. When my license was due for renewal the first time after I lost my hand, the procedure was almost a simple formality until the person behind the counter noticed that I had a motorcycle validation at the top of my old license. She said that they didn't issue cycle validations to people with one hand. I couldn't believe what she said. "Wait a minute; I've been operating it for a year and a half, and now you're telling me that I am not capable?" She hit a very touchy area with me. She said I could talk with the supervisor. He suggested that I write to the main office at the state capital explaining my situation, which I did promptly. I told them in no uncertain terms that I had been riding for years before my loss and a year after, with no problems and that I would not accept their present policy of refusing to issue a cycle validation to persons with one hand. I also mentioned something about letting my friends at the local TV station new departments know about this policy. I received a letter from the department saying that they decided to give me a cycle test on a certain date. I was overjoyed! That was all I wanted, a chance to prove that I was capable.

When I arrived at the lot where the test course was set up, I noticed that they had a group of observers in attendance. In addition to the people from the local office, and the usual cycle examiner, a state Motor Vehicle Department employee who also had a hook was waiting. They apparently brought him in from somewhere else in the state to act as a prosthetic expert for the Department of Motor Vehicles. I was put through the paces of a standard cycle operators test. I was asked to ride between pylons, make turns, arm signals and stop on a line. I accomplished these without any problems. The examiner who administered the test to me was quite friendly. I had the feeling he was on my side from the beginning. He said I passed and was free to go. I could sense a general feeling of irritation among the "official" observers. I don't know what they expected to see, but they were defeated and could do nothing but change the state policy and grant equal rights to all.

Getting back to some other household tasks, I find sewing, by hand or machine, isn't any more difficult than with two hands. You may want to do a bit of experimenting with new grasping techniques. I often use a machine to make small items, or modify my clothes. The hook aids in holding pieces of fabric together when running them through a machine. When threading a needle, either the hand or hook can be used to grasp the thread. Without the hook, simply stick the needle into something to hold it while threading.

Many hands and arms are lost in various kinds of farm machinery, especially clogged corn pickers. Aside from the discomfort of wearing a prosthesis on a ninety-degree summer day when bailing hay, the farmer's hook does a fine job of helping with the chores and other jobs. It is strong enough to assist the hand in lifting the heavy tongue onto the tractor hitch. One can lift as much or even more weight with the hook than a hand. The shell of my arm comes up over the end of my elbow with a lip. This prevents the arm from sliding off if the elbow is bent slightly. This enables me to use the strength of my whole arm and part of my upper body in the lifting process, instead of just the strength of my hand and wrist. The control cable which goes over my back and under my opposite arm brings my upper body into play also (as long as the ends of the cable do not pop off under the strain). Ray realizes that it is sometimes necessary to lift with super-human strength on the farm and tries to build this extra reserve into his prosthesis.

It would be impossible to describe all the types of construction jobs that can be accomplished with the aid of a prosthesis, but I will mention a few. The most basic, pounding a nail, is real easy. You simply grasp the nail with then of the farmer's hook (a groove is even provided for this purpose), place the nail in the desired area, and hit it with the hammer. If you miss, you won't feel a thing! The Dorrance number eight and 555 hooks cannot hold a nail. This is one of the reasons I dislike them for most chores. The farmers's hook will not allow you to pound a nail shorter than about 3/4 of an inch in length. It is sort of "swallowed up" in the holding process and nothing is left sticking out of the grasping area to pound. Often a small brad such as this can be simply pushed into the wood with the fingers, enough to make it stay there by itself, before pounding. I helped some friends put steel siding on a barn building one time, and found that I had difficulty with the short nails we were using. A tip sicks up, just behind the end of the hook where I held the nail, which I often hit instead of the nail head. I finally decided to cut this projection off. It wasn't nearly as important to me as was the ability to pound shorter nail. I'm not real sure what it is for, except that it often comes in handy for something. I have used my hook to pull nails too, by grasping them just as one would with a hammer, and prying them out. The farmer's hook does a good job of wheeling a wheelbarrow (this is beginning to sound like a commercial for the farmer's hook!). Doing heavy lifting is good exercise for the amputated arm, as it keeps the muscles from atrophying. Unless it is used in the manner every day, the end of it can become quite sore from the unusually heavy pressure of the skin against the ends of the amputated bones. It is best to gradually increase the work load, giving the arm time to recover in between. A callus, just like the one covering the elbow, will develop in the area with the most pressure against the bones. This will provide the needed protection for the arm.

I once met a fifteen-year-old boy who was living on a farm nearby. He had a left hook, a Dorrance number eight, and I had a right farmer's hook. We exchanged gloves, as we had opposite hands. The purchase of his prosthesis was funded by a local charity organization. He was very grateful for their assistance, but did not know anything about the kind of terminal device that might have been most useful to him. Unfortunately, he did not get a farmer's hook. Because I felt inadequate around my farm with my 555 hook, I often felt sorry for him. It just couldn't do the job.

Pushing wood through a table saw is one job that the prosthesis does very safely. You are not risking any live fingers. A can of paint can be pried open with the end of a hook, if you can't find a screwdriver. I wired a house with the aid of my hook. One must be careful around live circuits, however, the steel of the hook is a good conductor of electricity.

As you can see, virtually anything can be done with one hand and a hook, but wouldn't it have been wonderful if they could have saved the hand? I always thought so until I met Myron. His story caused me to think twice...

CHAPTER 7

They Saved His Hand

The last thing Myron remembered as he went into surgery was telling the doctor to save his hand. Now, five years later, he is not so sure it was such a good idea.

Myron worked for a feed mill in a small Wisconsin farm community. He was forty-four years old. He grew up on a farm and had always worked hard. One of his gravest fears as a boy was losing a limb in a farm accident. His parents had marital problems and eventually broke up. Myron had to move to an orphanage and then a foster home. Hard work was a source of satisfaction for Myron. He worked at a paper converting mill for ten years and enjoyed his work at the feed mill. He got to know the people in the community as he made his rounds to the farms in the area. Myron often worked eighteen to twenty hours a day in the spring. He decided to make one more delivery on this sunny day in July, before going home for lunch. As Myron was unloading ground feed at a nearby farm, the auger which carried the feed jammed up and stalled. He shut the hydraulic system off as he always did when he had problems like this, and put the gears in reverse so if it accidently started while he was working on it, the auger would turn in reverse. What he didn't know was that some pins in the drive mechanism had sheared and the auger was now free to turn. As he gradually freed the auger of feed, the pressure of the load on the auger caused it to suddenly rotate, drawing his hand into it before Myron realized what was happening. His hand was drawn into the auger, and he couldn't pull it out. His yells and screams were eventually heard by the farmer who was working nearby. The farmer alone could not turn the auger, so he called Myron's boss at the feed mill. He came right over, and together they were eventually able to rotate the auger enough to extract Myron's arm and severed hand.

Myron was taken to the University Of Wisconsin Medical School in Madison where it was felt the expertise needed to attempt to re-attach the hand could be found. Myron had known of a man in his hometown area that had his hand re-attached after an accident, and was able to return to work with good use of it. His foremost thought was that he wanted them to save his hand too. The doctors spent over nine hours restoring the blood circulation and tendons.

His first thought as he regained consciousness was, "What do I do now?" The next evening, the doctors informed him that they had to remove the hand again because of infection. There was still a chance the it might have to be amputated. However they were able to clean it out and successfully re-attach it once again. His hand was severed at the wrist joint, which made the process more difficult. a week later, the doctors came in for his check-up and asked him if he could move any of his fingers. To everyone's amazement, he could move his middle finger. At this, they thought he might regain sixty to seventy percent of its use. Unfortunately, it never improved past this stage.

Operations to improve his hand's movement continued. He has had twenty-three in all. He went to the Boston Medical Center for tests and more surgery. His hand was attached to his stomach for eighteen days on two different occasions over the years, in order to graft new skin over the area where they had operated. He has now reached the point where if he accidently injures the skin covering the area, he no longer has any skin left to replace it with. The hand will then have to be amputated. His thumb and wrist have been fused, which prevents movement, but he has adequate circulation and good feeling in the hand. He can sense hot and cold.

Myron attended technical school and obtained an associate degree in accounting. He has also been undergoing therapy at the Curative Rehabilitation Center in Green Bay to improve the mobility of his hand. During this time he has also been constantly battling infection. At present, he is unable to obtain employment because, when the question of his health arises during an interview, he must admit that a new case of infection could force him into the hospital at any time. With this possibility looming over his head, no one wants to hire him.

Myron has decided he won't allow any more operations on his hand. If he had been working last fall, he would have said no to the last surgery. He gets frustrated when he can't hold a hammer or nail with his hand. He said, "Doctor, save my hand," five years ago, when there was possibility of its being re-attached. He has wondered many times since, if that was the right decision. If he cuts it open, it won't heal and it will have to be amputated. "Maybe it would be a relief. Then I would at least know where I am at."

CHAPTER 8

The Six Million Dollar Man

(This chapter is about the first electric-mechanical hand made for the public. This information is over20 years old. Since then, there has been a lot of technology advances and this is now very outdated, but it is interesting to learn how this all started.)

About the same time this television series was popular in the mid-seventies, a new prosthetic device was beginning to be available in certain area across the U.S. It received much publicity by the press, probably because of the TV series which featured a fictional test pilot who was injured in a plane crash and subsequently rejuvenated by secret government prosthetic techniques, which apparently were worth six million dollars. He was shown with an electro-mechanical hand that was supposedly much stronger than the human hand it replaced. It allowed him to perform wondrous feats. The hand which was becoming available to the general public was made by the Otto Bock Company in West Germany. An American distribution facility was located in Minneapolis. It imported the components for these arms and trained prosthetist in the construction, fitting and maintenance of these custom made prostheses. When I learned of these new hands I talked to Ray, the prosthetist who made my mechanical arm and found out that none had been made up to that time in Wisconsin. He was interested in attending one of the seminars at Otto Bock in Minneapolis to learn the construction techniques, but needed a client that he could use to train on. After much deliberation about spending $3500 for a new arm, I decided to give it a try.

I had to take out a bank loan to pay for it. I reasoned that it was a matter of how much a hand was worth to the individual. As it had only been a few years since I lost my hand, it apparently still seemed quite valuable to me. The glamour of the Six Million Dollar Man may have had some bearing on my decision, although I'd never admit it. I had no idea how much use the hand would actually be, but since I have always been interested in new technology, I decided to give it a try.

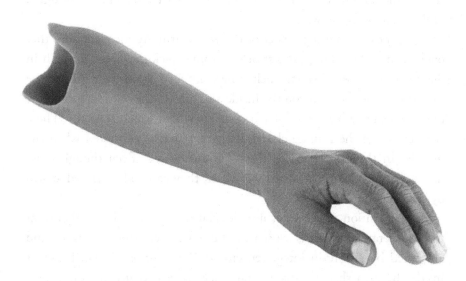

Ray and I drove across the state to the Bock plant. It was to be a three day session. They had a staff that was trained and ready to instruct certified prosthetists from all parts of the country in the techniques of making and fitting arms for the new "myo-electric" Otto Bock Hands. "Myo" refers to muscle. The hand wasn't actually "bionic". This would infer that it was actually combined with, and part of a living limb, which it was not. The prosthesis consists of a resin and cloth socket which is designed to fit the residual limb very closely. Into the end of this flesh colored shell, or "arm"

is molded a mechanical receptacle with three electrical slip rings which supply five volts of power to operate the hand. The power is supplied by a rechargeable battery that snaps into a compartment located on the inside of the arm shell.

The hand itself is quite a marvel of mechanical engineering. It is available in sizes ranging from child through men's large. It looks quite realistic because the mechanics of it is covered by a glove made of a flesh colored rubber material in the form of a replaceable glove. It had an inner mechanism made of aluminum that looks somewhat like a persons' own thumb and forefingers. The mechanism is driven by an electric motor, through a two-speed transmission and clutch. The function is a simple open-close movement. The two smaller fingers on the hand are made of rubber and simply follow the movement of the driven fingers, through a heavy piece of spring wire.

The most intriguing aspect of the whole arm are the electrodes that operate the hand. They consist of two round pickups, about an inch in diameter and one-half inch thick. These are held against the skin of the forearm by the shell, one on the inside and one on the outside, just below the elbow. They have gold-plated contacts which touch the skin. These contacts sense the minute electrical current that is generated when the muscles in the arm that flex the wrist are moved. Even though these muscles are no longer attached to a wrist, they can still be flexed at will by the user.

The flexation of the outer muscles causes a minute electrical current to be generated, which is sensed by the outside electrode contacts, and amplified by a built-in integrated circuit. This current is sent by wires inside the arm shell to a solid state switch located in the hand. This switch turns on the electric motor, causing the hand mechanism to be driven open. When the hand reaches its maximum open position, the clutch slips, allowing the motor to continue to turn as long as the muscle is flexed to produce the operating current. If the clutch were not part of the mechanism, the motor would stall when it reached its operating limit, and could be damaged electrically.

To close the hand, the muscles that used to bend the wrist inward are flexed. The current generated is picked up by the inner electrode and is sent to the hand switch. This causes the switch to reverse the current to the motor, causing it to operate in reverse, driving the hand closed until the flexation is stopped by the user. If no flexation occurs, no current is generated by the muscles and the hand remains motionless. A sensitivity control is mounted in each electrode so that the sensitivity of the amplifiers can be regulated. If the sensitivity is turned down, a large amount of flexation and resulting signal must be generated before the hand will respond. If the sensitivity is turned up, the slightest movement of the muscle is detected, resulting in hand movement when it is not consciously desired. We'll get back to more on the operation of the hand later.

The hand is held onto the arm by a "total contact" arm socket. This means the socket is designed to fit directly against the skin, very snugly. A close fit is necessary to ensure that the electrodes are always in contact with the skin. If this contact was lost because of a loose fit, the hand would not operate. The shell is designed to extend over the elbow a bit, which ensures that it will not fall off the arm under normal use. Straps are not used to hold the arm on. This makes it very comfortable to wear. However, while the arm inside the shell still gets hot in the summer, at least the upper body is not made uncomfortable by a harness.

Before construction of an arm is begun, the client is tested with a meter to determine if he or she is able to flex the arm muscles enough to produce sufficient current to operate the hand. This "myo" tester can also be used to help a person exercise a weak arm by providing an indication of how much current is generated during each flexation. As the muscles are flexed again and again, the output gradually increases. If the test is made soon after the loss of the hand, the meter will indicate that the muscles are still relatively strong. If the loss occurred several years before, the muscles probably have atrophied to some extent and need exercise to generate a useful current level. I was a bit weak at first, but within fifteen minutes, I was able to generate a sufficient signal. Often a bit of practice is needed to "re-educate" the muscles, because without a hand to move, they are not used. I was given a hand, battery and two electrodes, which were taped to my forearm. I went off by myself and practiced with it in order to become accustomed to the amount of flexation necessary to operate the Bock hand. It was a lot of fun to watch the hand open and close, as if by magic. The speed of its operation and the amount of squeeze is not variable. The motor is either running or stopped. I found that short bursts of power replaced a variable speed function. I could not, of course, feel how hard the hand was gripping an object, I had to watch the hand operate in order to adjust the amount of squeeze it had. This took a bit of practice but wasn't at all difficult.

Interestingly, the muscle movement one uses to operate the hand is flexation of the wrist forward and back which will close and open the hand. After a few weeks of use, my brain converted my mental command of "flex wrist inward" into "hand close". I soon forgot what these muscles did before I lost my hand and formed a new mental picture to control my new electric prosthesis. Then, after I used the myo arm for several weeks, I switched back to my body powered hook. I found that my brain was a bit confused. I would often extend my hook and flex my arm muscles as if I was going to open the electric hand. Needless to say, my hook didn't respond.

The actual construction of the arm is similar to that used with conventional or body powered arms with hooks. Because these prostheses do not use arm socks, the fit needs to me more exact.

After Ray finished my arm, I was free to return home. He stayed on for a few more days of instruction and I caught a cab to the airport that afternoon. I felt very strange with a hand on the end of my right arm after all these years of using a hook. I felt as if everyone was looking at me as I stood in line to check in. Logically, I had no reason to be concerned--the hand looked quite natural. Maybe I was worried that I would forget how to flex my muscles and that the hand might refuse to open. It was that old familiar routine of the fear of failure and of feeling foolish in front of others. I made it home with out any problems, and I doubt that anyone was even aware of my new "six million dollar" hand.

Accomplishing daily activities was now a new adventure for me. I also felt different--more like others, now that I had two hands. I believe the main reason an amputee will spend thousands of dollars for this type of prosthesis is because it looks more natural than a hook. Secondly, it can perform a useful function on the end of the arm and it is more comfortable to wear than an arm with a harness.

It looks quite natural--from the wrist down to the fingertips. Above the wrist, where the rubber glove ends, it is flesh colored, but definitely looks like an artificial arm. While wearing a short sleeved shirt, this appearance can bother some wearers. I once saw a college student who was wearing myo arm, and was apparently quite concerned about his appearance, because he had his arm wrapped in an ace bandage from just above his wrist to above his elbow, where the plastic of the arm ended. This was his way of hiding the arm, in an attempt to make it look more acceptable to his world. When Peter first began to wear his prosthesis, you may remember that he always wore a long sleeved shirt in order to hide it. I also feel a bit strange when I wear a short sleeved shirt for the first time in the spring. This feeling is quite common, but affects some people more than others. This depends on one's level of self-worth and confidence. I go through this same period of concern about appearance in the summer when it's too hot to wear any type of prosthesis and I go to work with my amputated arm exposed. I find that my feelings of self-consciousness only lasts as short time, however. Feeling O.K. about one's self when wearing a prosthesis is a very important concern among those of us who must wear one. The appearance of the myo hand and its function, as basic as it may be, is perhaps enough reason to justify its high cost.

Let's take a closer look at the function and usefulness of the myo-electric hand. Because of the aluminum fingers, somewhat fragile gear mechanism and skin-like rubber glove, it is not a prosthesis that can be used for heavy work, or work that involves heat, inks, paints, stains and sharp edges. These all will damage the glove. As of this writing, a glove cost about $85. Any one of the above hazards can cause enough damage to necessitate replacement of the glove, or worse, require repair of the drive mechanism inside--this is the voice of experience speaking. Recently I tripped on a crack in the sidewalk while walking up to the entrance of a theatre. I naturally reached out with both hands to break my fall, and broke a part in my electric hand at the same time. This trip cost me $75 and it was three weeks before I had the use of my hand again.

Let me discuss the function of the myo electric hand as I go about my daily activities. The rechargeable battery now costs about $150. It will power the hand for about eight hours when new. My first set of batteries lasted three years, before their useful life diminished to about four or five hours. This was not long enough to get me through the average work day, and I had to replace them. The recharge cycle takes about twelve hours.

This necessitates having two batteries, so that one can be charging, while the other is in use. If I plan to be away from home until late at night, I must take the spare battery and its charger with me to work, and change batteries late in the afternoon. The discharge rate depends upon the activity of the user. I find if I sit around a lot during the day, one battery will last until I retire at night. On the other hand, I find that if I am very active, ride my cycle, type, etc., the battery will run down sooner.

Although the hand can easily grasp a glass at the breakfast table, I don't usually use it for this purpose. If I were to inadvertently flex my muscles the wrong way, the hand could open and drop the glass. A power switch located inside the palm of the myo hand can be used to turn the power off so that this cannot happen. The hand will continue to hold the object until he switch is again turned on. However, this short-term use of the power switch is not practical. It was meant for long-term grasp protection, such as holding a cocktail glass at a party.

Because the hand is covered by a skin-like rubber glove, one must be careful around hot items in the kitchen. The rubber/plastic material will melt. It works well for grasping a sponge when doing dishes, and you can clean the glove with the sponge before you drain the sink. It does a good job around the kitchen when holding things like vegetables for slicing. I usually use the myo hand to steady or grasp objects, such as holding a toothbrush, and let my real hand do the finer work of squeezing the toothpaste tube from the bottom.

The myo hand has difficulty picking up objects because it will not flex at the wrist and the movement of the fingers is rather primitive. Instead, I use my real hand to pick up the object, place it in my myo hand, and then proceed to work on it while the myo hand does the easy job of grasping the object.

The rubber glove allows one to grasp a door knob, but because of the lack of wrist movement, the knob cannot easily be twisted. Otto Bock does offer a wrist rotation feature, but I've never seen one in use, and suspect the added weight and power requirements may not be worth the small use that is gained. If the doorknob rotates easily, the open hand itself can often be slid down the side of the knob, causing it to rotate enough to open the door. It is unfortunate that America does not use the lever-type knobs that are common in Europe. Round knobs present numerous, frustrating and unnecessary problems to those without hands. The library where I work has smooth, slippery little round knobs on every door. If I ever meet the architect who specified these aesthetically pleasing, but impossible-to-twist knobs, I would love to enlighten him on the problems he created.

The myo hand does a good job of operating the shift lever in a car, and can grasp the steering wheel easily. It also holds the handlebar grip on bicycles nicely. I would hesitate to do anything that involves heavy jarring, such as using a splitting mall, sledge hammer or maybe even a baseball bat. Sooner or later the forces involved in these activities will bend the fingers and strain or even break the drive gears. One could shovel light, fluffy snow, but not the wet, heavy stuff. The load of a shovel can be lifted by the real hand and the myo hand can be used on the upper end of the shovel, but I find this allows the shovel to twist and rotate easily, often dumping the load. I wouldn't recommend carrying pails of water with it, or even thinking of lifting bales of hay. This is what the farmer's hook was designed for. Use the myo hand when you go to town on Saturday night.

Although I can type reasonably well with my myo hand, using the thumb to hit the keys, I find the hand does not want to stay wide open for long. It soon begins to close, requiring the use of the motor to open it again. This is an almost constant drain on the battery. Also, some typewriters are designed in such a way that the fingers of the hand constantly hit the front of the typewriter's cover. This prevents one from typing at all unless the cover is lifted, as when the ribbon is changed. A lightweight hook really work better here.

I wouldn't get too involved in auto mechanics with the hand because the rubber glove can be easily cut or stained. The same holds true in the shop. Farmer's hooks are virtually indestructible allowing the user to forget about the prosthesis and get to work!

In summary, the myo electric hand looks quite natural, and is more comfortable to wear than the body-powered hook. Technological advances in electronics and integrated circuits will eventually result in hands that will give us sensory feedback and have more sophisticated finger movements. Today's hands are not, however, durable enough for heavy work. They are expensive to purchase and maintain. For those who are concerned about appearance, the myo hand is at the top of the list of devices available to amputees who also want some function.

A friend of mine, Dick, is having a prosthesis built with a myo hand on it. He will be using it mostly for social events. But, maybe I'm getting ahead of myself. I should start at the beginning of his story...

CHAPTER 9

"...I had to pull my arm off."

After high school, he went to work in a logging camp for a year-and-a-half. Then he drove a semi-truck for nine months and got laid off. He didn't have any particular goal in mind when he was hired at the cheese plant. Dick's job was to tear down the heavy equipment that was used in a cheese processing plant to grind up 500 pound blocks for reprocessing. He dismantled the machines, then cleaned and sterilized them with steam. He was a maintenance man on the night shift and was twenty years old.

On this fateful night Dick was working alone in the room with the machine. Other maintenance people were scattered throughout the building. For some unexplainable reason, the machine started up and the auger began to pull him in. First it tore four fingers off of his left arm.

"When it got to above my elbow, I pulled my arm off--the next cut would have been my shoulders and head," he recalled uncomfortably.

His main thought was to get out of the room he was in and get to a hospital. "I ran around the floor I was on carrying what was left of my arm, looking for someone. I didn't feel any pain at the time."

One of the other workers on the floor tackled him and took his t-shirt off and wrapped it around the end of what was left of his left arm. He then tied a knot in it, took his screwdriver out of his belt, put it through the knot and twisted it to stop the bleeding.

"As I laid there, my whole life seemed to flash before me. I saw a lot of things that I did right and wrong," Dick said. "One of the rescue squad men said they were just in time, I didn't have much blood left."

At the hospital, Dick told them not to call his wife. She was pregnant with their first baby, and was a week and a half overdue. They called his brother, who went over to their house and got her.

One of his first thoughts as he lay there was that his wife might not want him with one arm gone. This proved to be very wrong. She had the baby four days later, a girl. His wife and new baby became his source of strength.

"When the baby was born, I knew I had responsibilities. I couldn't let it get to me. I was more mad than anything."

Dick didn't feel sorry for himself but did get down at times.

He found that alcohol was very depressing, "...and I still felt terrible the next morning. I found it didn't do any good."

Because his hand and arm were badly torn up, there was no possibility of reattaching it. He was left with a stump about six inches long. After being in the hospital one week, he became very frustrated and told the doctor, "You can't do anything for me that I can't do for myself at home." He was anxious to get back into the world with his wife and new baby daughter and begin experimenting with getting along with one arm.

Dick came from a family of six children. They were all very close. He would often get phone calls from them when one or the other would discover new ways of accomplishing the things he did before his loss. One of his married brothers even went so far as to have his wife tie his left arm behind his back, and spent a whole day working about the house discovering the problems and frustrations his younger brother was encountering. His family had a very positive and helpful attitude, yet maintained the position that, "If you want something, you better work for it." His dad always said that his children had to learn to work.

During his recovery he kept active. One of his younger brothers would come over and shoot baskets with him, finding new ways to play with one arm. He learned how to tie his shoes with one hand, but could never seem to get them tight enough. Washing dishes was hard at first.

Dick was fitted with a prosthesis about two months after his accident. Because Dick's arm is only about six inches long below his shoulder, his stump fits into a socket or shell, to which the rest of the arm is attached. This shell then allows the short arm inside enough leverage to move the attached prosthesis about. A mechanical elbow with a forearm lift-assist was used. This is a locking elbow with the addition of a spring mechanism which makes it easier for Dick to raise the forearm section of the arm independently.

Operation of the arm requires three independent movements. One to raise the forearm, one to lock it into the desired position, and one to open the terminal device. The raising movement and opening of the terminal device is accomplished with the same movement. This involves the shrugging of the shoulders, which pulls on the control cable attached to the terminal device. With the elbow locked in a fixed position, the terminal device is opened by this pull. The forearm's locking mechanism is operated by a short cable connected to a chest strap. By moving the whole arm sideways, away from the body with the stump inside the socket at the top of the prosthesis, the elbow mechanism is locked and unlocked. Only about 2 inches of sideways movement is necessary to activate the lock. It is a pull-lock, pull-unlock action. The shoulder shrug movement then either lifts the arm to the desired height or opens the terminal device. This may all sound a bit complicated, but actually it becomes quite a simple technique after it is tried a few times.

Because the forearm must be lifted by the pull of a cable with straps across the back, and under the opposite arm, the weight of the prosthesis below the point of the elbow must be kept to a minimum. In this situation the 555 aluminum hook is ideal because of its light weight. If physical labor is to be performed, a farmer's hook may be more appropriate, but because it is made of steel, it is quite heavy. This added weight becomes a burden towards the end of a working day. The excessive weight of some mechanical hands may make their use with mechanical elbows prohibitive. Dick says that the weight of a can of pop is about the maximum amount that he can lift without undue strain. This is why he favors using the aluminum hook.

In actual daily use, the arm with the prosthesis is not generally the one that does any amount of lifting work. It would not, for instance, be the arm that would lift a shovel full of snow. Instead, the prosthesis would be used to grip the end of the shovel handle to steady it and the good arm would do the actual lifting of the load. If a bale of hay were to be lifted, the prosthesis could be used, but the elbow should be in a straight-down position. This relieves the elbow locking mechanism of excessive strain. The lifting force would then be generated with the good arm and the shoulder of the prosthetic arm, with the straps bearing most of the load. The amount that can be lifted is dependent upon the type of terminal device in use and how much strain the cable and end fitting can withstand. The cables themselves and the straps are not likely to break, but the fittings at the ends that make the connection to the straps are the weak points. They are either soldered or crimped to the ends of the cables. Eventually the stainless steel cables begin to fray at these connection points and will pop at the most inopportune time. I had this happen while skiing in Vermont one year. It was the connection across my back that broke. Just as they say, "Out of sight, out of mind," I couldn't see that it was getting weak.

Dick soon found that he could still do almost everything he did before, it just took a bit longer and often required more patience. He still plays basketball and football. He was often called upon to manage local baseball teams but eventually got tired of watching the fun and wanted to play himself. Now he goes for a base hit instead of a home run. He works on his own vehicles, rating his ability with his prosthesis at about ninety percent.

"I use my hook mostly for holding things while my good hand does the real work. When you look at it this way, it's no big deal," Dick commented.

To my surprise, I found that Dick doesn't like to wear short sleeved shirts when he has his arm on. I assumed that anyone with his level of confidence would not be self-conscious about allowing his arm to be seen by others. However, he related that because of the additional cable and hardware at his artificial elbow, he thought it looked too mechanical and might be offensive to some people. He felt that his arm was "a personal thing" and was more comfortable with a long sleeved shirt rolled up a bit.

Dick and I both have the same feeling, however, about hot weather and prosthetics--they don't go well together. He doesn't always wear his arm around the house unless he is going to work on some specific project that makes its use necessary. He will steady or hold things with his feet and knees or even in his teeth.

"People are sometimes afraid to ask me to do things when I don't have my arm on. I think they should ask, and if I think I can't do it, I'll tell them."

Even though Dick had a new arm, his problems were far from over. The cheese company where the accident occurred originally assured him that they would have a job for him when he recovered. He got off workman's compensation early so that he could get his life back together and continue working, "instead of moping around."

He recalled that, "You've got to make it happen yourself, because no one else is going to do it for you."

With renewed enthusiasm he was ready to again support his new family, but he soon had the wind knocked out of his sails. "The biggest downer out of the whole experience was that there was no job for me when I went back. They said they didn't feel that I could do any of the jobs that were there. I asked them to at least let me try my old job with my new artificial limb, but they said no."

The doctor's report in the release that permitted him to return to work contained the usual generalities regarding precautionary recommendations that suggested he refrain from heavy lifting and have sufficient rest periods during the work day. In ordinary medical terms, this may sound fine, but when one knows and considers Dick's enthusiasm and ability for hard work, it becomes clear that these restrictions don't apply. "I found I could lift more than ever before. That hook is much stronger than a hand," he added. Company promises of managerial positions never materialized.

Determined to support his own family, he trapped wild game and fished for a year because they had no income. They lived on $57 a week. "As long as I could still get out there and do something I wouldn't let my parents pay the way. They were very supportive."

With the help of the State Department of Vocational Rehabilitation, he went to technical school and obtained a degree in marketing and transportation. He went on to take courses in business administration at the University. "I still had a need to work while in school. I felt kind of rotten collecting money while in school. I wanted to get out and do something."

Dick was able to find part-time work cleaning up at the orthopedic shop which happened to be located in the same building below their apartment. He even swept floors at the Teamsters hall after meetings. In the summer he mowed lawns and in winter he shoveled sidewalks, apparently completely forgetting about the medical restrictions.

"There were several other guys at tech school with disabilities. Everyone thought that we'd be the first ones to get jobs when we got out. Actually one of the guys that had a leg off did get a job right away, but he didn't last long. He was let go in a few months; he had a really bad attitude and outlook on life."

Dick sent out 125 resumes after graduation, and was able to obtain 44 job interviews.

I applied at a lumber yard where they advertised for someone to check in loads of wood. There wasn't any physical work involved. All you had to do was go around with a clip board."

As he left the building, he saw the interviewer throw his application in the waste basket, "Boy, that was a downer! I found out that being handicapped does not help you get a job."

It was three months before Dick was able to find work. He didn't think that his qualifications prevented him from being hired previously.

"I think I got this first job because the employer got a tax write-off for hiring a handicapped person." An electrical warehouse nearby was apparently losing money, and the prospect of a tax incentive was enough to prompt them to hire Dick.

Not only did the company save tax money by hiring Dick, but they soon began to turn a profit through his excellent management skills.

"I put in many long hours there. I was so glad to have a job at last that I really didn't care how long I worked."

Dick got his present job mainly because of his attitude. He struck up a conversation with a man seated next to him at a football came one Sunday afternoon. Their conversation eventually got around to his arm and the problems he had finding work. The man was impressed with Dick's attitude despite the may hardships he had encountered since his loss.

"I was crazy then, and I'm crazy now," he joked. "The loss of my arm didn't change my outlook!"

Dick soon received a phone call from a large wholesale food distributor. After an interview and wage negotiations he was hired as a front line supervisor to manage a warehouse and 68 workers.

Dick told me, "I feel an outgoing personality can really save the situation in a job interview. You need to make the interviewer feel comfortable with your problem. People don't always know what to say to you. When they hear you joke about it and can see it doesn't bother you, everything gets back to normal. I found out I had to break the ice. Our society is geared to a persons appearance and if you aren't a perfect person, then you're going to have a problem. If you can convince the employer to give you a chance at the job--to just let you try it, then you have a chance. So often it seems that the interviewer himself has a personal hang-up in dealing with the handicapped. Too often it's not a company policy that prevents you from getting the job, but the interviewer who personally feels awkward. In reality, a handicapped person usually gives 100% because jobs are so scarce. They appreciate being able to work--much more than most people. I know I do..."

CHAPTER 10

Life Without Hands

Thus far in out journey though the world of "One Handers" we've always had the use of at least one good hand. Now we shall learn what life is like when all of one's prehensile agility is lost. We will learn the stories of two people, one who lost his hand within the last eight years, and the other forty years ago.

Wayne

Wayne had always been an active kid. He and his year-older brother were "always raising hell". He quit high school in his junior year and went to work for a construction firm--more physical activity. He was working with his brother, erecting steel buildings. Tragedy struck them on a damp, soggy morning. Four men were moving a tall aluminum scaffold into place to continue work on a new steel building when suddenly an electric arc jumped from a nearby 7200 volt powerline to the metal scaffold that they were holding. In a flash, two co-workers were killed and the two brothers were badly injured. Wayne was unconscious and his brother was badly burned, but coherent. He thought Wayne was dead along with the others on the ground. Despite his burned feet and hands, Wayne's brother managed to crawl to their truck, climb inside, and get the engine started. He went for help.

Wayne and his brother were taken 100 miles south to the Milwaukee

Burn Center. There wayne drifted in and out of consciousness for over ten days. He had been married only six months earlier. When at last he was able to understand what had happened to him, he learned that his brother had suffered severe burns on his feet and had to have one hand amputated. His other hand would ultimately be saved, but would remain a crippled claw. Wayne's feet were badly burned, causing the loss of his little toes on both feet. He still had both hands, but they were also badly burned. Electrical burns differ from fire burns in that the worst damage often occurs on the inside beneath the skin and cannot be readily seen. This is somewhat like the effects of microwave cooking. In contrast, fire affects the outside layers of skin first. Only time would tell the ultimate extent of damage. With both his hands and feet burned and bandaged, he was totally helpless.

As he lay there in constant pain he wondered why it had happened to him. His fellow workers were dead, his own brother was crippled, but at least alive.

"I wondered how I would support my new wife. I wondered what use I would be to anyone without hands."

His mind was obsessed with these concerns as he lay in bed, day after day. His hands were swollen and painful--he dare not try to move them. The doctors were doing their best to save his hands; he had numerous skin grafts, but each time a graft would fail, more dead skin had to be removed, leaving less and less flesh to cover the bones.

Wayne suffered mentally and physically for a month and a half, totally helpless in the hospital bed, waiting and wondering.

"I felt like a newborn baby--I couldn't do anything for myself. My wife was a cook in a restaurant back home. She would come down and visit me on weekends."

Problems with his hands continued.

"Their main arteries would often break and had to be sewn up. There wasn't enough flesh left in my hands to support the artery walls."

When the artery in his left hand broke again the doctor told the nurse to stitch it up once more.

Wayne said, "I thought it would be alright again. They said I was gong down for surgery but they didn't say what for. When I came out of the anesthetic I realized that my hand was gone--they couldn't save it."

Three days later when the artery broke in his right hand, he knew when they said he'd be gong down for surgery that his other hand would have to go also.

"I'm glad they did," he said in retrospect, "I wouldn't want to have to live with two crippled hands."

Wayne had deep burns in the area of both wrists. They amputated both hands just about the wrists, leaving him quite helpless. His wife felt that she now had to take care of him for the rest of his life. Wayne recalled his wife's feeding him.

"One of the biggest hassles with this was how to tell her that I had enough to drink."

Now, with both of his damaged hands gone, the pain began to subside as his arms began to heal. A prosthetist came in and instructed the hospital staff on how to wrap the ends of his arms. This was important in order to ensure that the swelling would subside as quickly as possible and allow him to be cast for prostheses. While in the hospital, he had the use of a device that could be slipped over the end of one of his bandaged arms, which would allow him to hold an eating utensil. This was the first time since the accident that he was able to do something for himself.

Two months after he got out of the hospital, he was cast for new arms. It took longer than usual for the swelling to subside.

"Gradually the phantom limb sensations died down. I had sharp, stabbing pains that seemed to explode in my hands, (which were, of course, gone) but they gradually disappeared over a few years."

Mentally he accepted the fact that his hands were gone, but the phantom sensations told him otherwise.

"It drove me nuts, it felt like my hands were still there. I often had sharper pains that related to various parts of my hands."

Wayne can still feel his hands, and make a fist with them, but it isn't painful as it was in the beginning.

His prostheses are generally identical to mine, as described in chapter five. There are two distinct differences, however. The first, and most obvious, is the fact that he has two of them. The control cable from the right hook is connected to the cuff of the left arm, and vice-versa.

Secondly, the hard shell portion of each arm that the hook screws into, does not extend up and over the end of his elbow to provide lifting power. When he lifts, the weight is supported by the straps that hold the prostheses onto his upper body, not by the arms inside of them. Some feel that having the lip on the end of the arm shell is uncomfortable. I'll admit that it is for the first two or three weeks. This lip is putting pressure on the back of the elbow where it has never been felt before. However, in amount or two, this tenderness will gradually go away as the elbow area becomes acclimated. After this initial "break-in" period has passed, the pressure can no longer be felt. From then on, the user has the advantage of being able to use his arm itself to lift with. Without the lip, all the weight is supported by the straps over the shoulder and across the back. This strain can be quite uncomfortable as the straps dig into your flesh. The lip on the end of the arm can be used to relieve either all or part of this strain, depending on how much the arm is bent. As the forearm is straightened out, permitting the arm inside to slide out of the shell, the load shifts from the arm to the straps across the back. I often change the distribution of my load purposely from one to the other while carrying for an extended time in order to be more comfortable. I personally like the lip, but arms are made both ways. If one is aware of this option, then there is a choice.

Wayne gets into his arms by laying them out in front of him, thrusting his arms into the shells and then lifting them up above his head, and allowing the harness assembly to slide down and across his back. He uses conventional white cotton socks on his arms instead of the specially knit wool prosthetic socks. His prosthetist suggested that they were expensive and not worth buying. I know others who also use conventional "foot" socks on their arms. This is another area where personal preference may prevail. I do feel, however, that there is little dispute over the fact that the special wool socks offer more cushioning and will absorb more perspiration than thinner cotton socks, and will almost last for ever. From there it is a matter of personal choice again.

Wayne's first prostheses had the flexation type wrist units installed in both arms, which he didn't like. They became loose and sloppy after they began to wear from heavy use. He didn't feel the extra flexation angle of the hooks was necessary. He is currently using one number 5X and one number 5 hook. The neoprene lining on the 5X is convenient for certain tasks. He must, however, have the rubber replaced several times a year due to heavy use. He has both arms resurfaced about twice a year also.

This process renews the exterior of the arms, and makes them look like new again.

After about three years, Wayne lost weight and had another pair of arms made. These fit snugly once again. He also had standard compression ring, non-flexing wrist units installed. He has had two farmer's hooks from the beginning, but never used them. He feels comfortable with he number fives. In the summer when it is warm, he wears his arms under his shirts, directly against his skin. Although he did receive some burns on his back from the accident, they have healed and do not pose a problem. He did not like the feeling of the harness on his back in the beginning. His prosthetist told him that he wouldn't notice it after a while, but he still finds it irritating at times, especially when the weather is hot.

After being fitted with two new prostheses he went to the hospital down the street from his prosthetic shop for training in the use of his limbs. Over the course of five sessions he learned how to write again and how to do difficult things, like pick up objects. Wayne has some definite opinions about his rehabilitation.

"The medical staff at the hospital was great, they really took good care of us, but they should have had a counselor come in from day one to explain how difficult it would be and what we could expect. Various people with one or both hands off came in to talk to me. There was a fifteen-year-old guy who came in who had two hooks, but hearing his story didn't seem to help. We didn't get much rehabilitation there."

Both Wayne and his wife had difficulty dealing with his loss, "My problems began when I was in the hospital. I became accustomed to having everything done for me, and eventually I began to depend on it. After I was released and went home, I depended on my wife. She felt she had to protect and take care of me because she didn't want me to get hurt again."

It also took Wayne about three years to get over the fear of an electrical shock. Eventually this dependency became a burden and they were divorced.

Finding another girl became a challenge for him. He needed to find out if his hooks would bother them. He lived with two room mates, who shared the rent. Actually he wasn't afraid to do things by himself. He admitted that he was using his wife as a crutch. Now that he was on his own, he found that he had to become self-sufficient. He began to develop more patience when doing things without his wife's help.

He says, "It doesn't pay to get mad, because it doesn't get you anywhere."

With the help of the DVR, he attended technical school where he studied to be an automotive parts specialist. Eventually he met his second wife.

"She didn't like my hooks at first, but as we got to know each other better, she liked me more and more," he recalled. "She doesn't baby me. We both enjoy fixing up our house. We work together by aren't so dependent on each other as I used to be."

Wayne likes to crack jokes about his abilities with his hooks. Over the years he lost the bitterness he once had. He looked for a job for over a year after he graduated. The parts house where he had his on-the-job training thought he did a good job, but when it was time to go back to apply for employment, they didn't have an opening.

Wayne said, "Employers look at what you HAVE first; they don't seem to care what you can DO. Two hooks don't look good to most people."

Wayne now has a part time job as a rural letter carrier.

"I like working outdoor and driving through the countryside. I fish and bow hunt. I got my first deer last year."

He also works for a local newspaper, supervising fifty carriers.

At home things are gong well with his new wife. Door knobs still frustrate him, but he is discovering many shortcuts that make life easier for him. He now buttons his shirts part way up before putting them on. Then he uses a button hook, which he made himself, to finish buttoning them up after he has them on. In the winter he prefers to wear sweaters and a vest. He finds these easier to manage than coats. Evidence of his hooks can be found around the house; cabinets and drawers have scratch marks near the handles from his hooks. In the kitchen he still has difficulty handling large cans, such as those that V-8 Juice comes in. Large glass pickle jars are also tricky.

As I watched him open his tool box, his efforts with two hooks felt rather clumsy to me, even though I use a hook myself. Watching someone else work with hooks gives me totally different feelings than when I do it. Suddenly I began to understand ho others felt about me. Wayne and I both feel very comfortable doing everyday tasks with hooks. We don't give it a second thought, it feels very normal to us. He sorted through the wrenches and screwdrivers in the top tray, by pushing them aside with his hooks. For the first time in my life I realized that I felt I wanted to help this person, just as other people have felt when they watched me work with my hook. I can understand why they may have felt awkward at times around me.

Wayne enjoys working with his shop tools. He couldn't get along without his table and band saws, and has found the battery-powered variable speed drill to very useful.

"They do a good job of turning screws and getting them started. It is hard to turn a regular screwdriver with my hooks."

Wayne and I stood in the driveway of his home as I was leaving. He thrust both hooks into the pockets of his jeans, just as other people often get comfortable by putting their hands in their pockets, and said, "I hate the word 'handicapped'; it's all in the head!"

Earl

Earl was twenty-one years old when he was aboard a Navy ship in the Pacific. It was August 1945. A forty millimeter shell exploded aboard ship and shredded both of his hands.

"I knew right away they were both gone for good," he told me. "Back home, my mother had a dream the night before my accident, that I lost both hands, and told the rest of the family about it at breakfast the next morning. When a telegram arrived at the house, she knew what the message was about."

He was flown via hospital plane to the Navy medical center in Valejo, California. Of the 800 amputees in the hospital, he found four others that had also lost both hands. He had recovered from the original surgery in a few months but had to return to surgery for a "revision", a nice medical term for having to do it again. The first surgery left him with both wrists. Ideally an arm prosthesis is more successful when the amputation is just above the wrist. The prosthesis becomes too long when the wrist is still intact, and the "buldge" of the wrist at the end of the person's arm presents a fitting problem to the prosthetist. The Navy doctors shortened both of his arms to allow the use of more ideal prosthetic techniques.

His stay in the hospital was extended to over thirteen months by an officer who wanted to use a cineplasty procedure on Earl. This is a technique where a tunnel is made in the biceps muscle of the arm to allow a large steel pin to be inserted in the muscle. To this pin was connected the control cable of the prosthesis, which pulled the terminal device open when the muscle is flexed. This was an alternate technique used to replace the strap under the opposite arm as a means of control. The tunnel in the arm muscle posed possible problems for the amputee. This control technique is not generally used now. Earl was given several leaves where he returned to Wisconsin to visit his family while he was "considering" this operation. Each time he returned to the hospital he refused to give his consent.

Deep inside, Earl had the feeling that people looked upon him as "some sort of freak". His fear was dispelled one night when he was taken out to a bar by some of his buddies from the hospital. He drank from his beer glass which he held with the stubs of both arms. He had a great time with his friends but suffered the next day from over-indulgence. That night seemed to "break the ice" for Earl and he lost his fear of being in public.

New arms were finally made for him and even new hands of aluminum. They were light in weight with all five fingers controlled by steel wires. They were covered with realistic rubber gloves that looked like skin. Earl found them to be aesthetically attractive, but not practical. He immediately favored the use of two steel hooks, which he still uses today.

The crew of my navy ship collected $5,000. They gave it to me when I was in the hospital. When I came back to Wisconsin I used the money to buy a big truck."

He was offered a job by his former boss, hauling milk, in five gallon cans, to the dairy. This involved loading the cans onto the truck, two or three times a day. Earl was born on a farm and was accustom to hard work. The loss of both hands did not prevent him from doing manual labor. With his truck he loaded and hauled eighty pound bags of fertilizer, twenty-four tons a day, and all by hook!

When Earl's drivers license was due for renewal in 1951, he went for his test in his car which had an automatic transmission. As he talked to the examiner, he remembered that his truck had a five-speed transmission with a two-speed rear end.

"In order to be licensed to drive the truck, I had to test in it. So I drove my car home and got it. After the test was over, the examiner said that he was supposed to give me a restricted license, but he didn't know what to restrict. He said I drove very well. I had to back up the length of an alley by looking into the two rear-view mirrors. After the examiner thought a minute, he wrote, "Must wear artificial hand while driving."

In 1966 he became the manager of the feed mill he worked for. During the course of a day he had to mix and bag feed and operated tractors around the plant. Over the years he has hauled hay, bailer twine, rafters, machinery, lumber, and sunflower seeds (which he had to shovel by hand, each nine ton load!).

Earl found, as Wayne had, that his first flexation wrist units weren't strong enough. The cables and rings on his prostheses wear holes in the arms of his shirts very quickly. At home he has octagon knobs on all the doors in his house, which he can manage with his hooks. His hooks have neoprene rubber on the insides of them. He uses six rubber bands for closing power, which provides a hefty grip. In the morning he finds dressing a hassle, so he has his wife button his shirts. For fun he likes to hunt and fish. He has special rings welded onto his shotguns which enable him to grip them more easily. The trigger guards are also modified for his hook. Wrenches frustrate him, although he has developed lots of patience.

Earl is now retired. He hurt his back lifting too much weight.

When one thinks about the loss of both hands, it is almost always assumed that the amputee would seek employment in office-type environments and avoid heavy work because of the disability. Earl is living proof that this isn't necessarily so!

CHAPTER 11

The Intentional Amputation

"Cut off your hand on purpose? You're CRAZY! Why would anyone want to do that?" I would expect most people to react this way. But it is a little known fact that there are thousands (the exact number is unknown) of individuals in all parts of the world who desire to be minus part or all of a limb. They are not "crazy" but seem to be afflicted by a condition which is just becoming recognized. At the time I did my hand I had no idea why I wanted this, other than it felt right. My feelings had not been identified or recognized as any particular type of disorder. I did not understand my feelings, or understand why I wanted to be minus my hand until I recently read about this desire in the book, "Amputee Identity Disorder: information, questions, answers, and recommendations about self-demand amputation," by Greg M. Furth, Ph.D. & Robert Smith, ChM, FRCSEd, (2002.) You may also visit the website, http://www.biid.org/BIID%20 Basics.htm

Obviously there can be numerous reasons for wanting to be minus a limb. In my case, I think it may have been a combination of several situations; my encountering an amputee at a young age in a supermarket, then later in life making friends with my neighbor Pete, who showed me that amputation could be alright given the right attitude. In my particular case, this may have served to reinforce my long-standing desire to become an amputee.

This amputation desire is being called Amputee Identity Disorder, or AID. As of this writing this condition is just now being recognized and studied further. Little has been written about it. Suddenly much of what I have been feeling for many years made sense!

At the same time, I began to receive feedback from writing the first addition of this book and an abbreviated version which I submitted to the website http://secretgardenstories.org/club.htm. Through this website I discovered that there were many people such as myself, who wanted to be minus a limb. This condition can affect gay and straight, male and female individuals. They come from all walks of life, and live in all parts of the world.

Let me tell you about some of these whom I met. Hopefully this will further your understanding of this condition. None of these people have come out or have gone public about their desire. It is not acceptable at this time. I have changed their names and their origins to preserve their privacy.

"Sam" contacted me by e-mail with a few questions after reading my story on the internet. He intentionally chopped off the end of one of his fingers as a teenager. He has always had the desire to loose his hand but could never bring himself to do it. My book gave him renewed energy in this direction. He was a very successful business man and was well known and respected in his community. He and his partner lived in an expensive home. His life couldn't have been better, except for his desire to be one-handed. He confided in me via e-mail, by telephone and eventually we met in person. We discussed how he could fake an accident to loose his hand. The actual act of losing the hand wasn't as difficult as the task of how to stage the accident so his many friends would believe him. He hadn't even expressed his desire to his partner which further complicated the task.

Eventually we stopped corresponding. I suspect that he could not bring himself to do it, in spite of his burning desire to be come one-handed. He expressed this over and over to me in our conversions, but could not find a way to have a convincing accident, or explain why it might have been surgically removed. He even considered flying to a foreign country where such procedures can be had in hospitals and clinics. Money wasn't an issue for him. But the problem of explaining it to the people back home always came up.

Then there is "Frank," who first encountered an amputee when he was about five. The man who came to clean their furnace every year had a hook, which he remembered clearly. Most of us who have the AID seem to recall seeing an amputee at an early age. Frank has wanted to be an amputee ever since. He told me that this desire has made life very difficult for him over the years and may have been a contributing factor in his marriage failure. He never expressed his amputation desire to his wife.

After reading my story he eventually gathered enough courage to write to me under an assumed name and e-mail address, and then to telephone me. He used a fictitious name, as he was very concerned about his amputation desire becoming known. I was the only person he ever confided in. As an engineer, he was worried about becoming incapacitated and not being able to support himself if he were to have only one hand. He lived in a rural area and was physically very active. Long before he contacted me, he constructed his own working prosthesis. He bound his hand up inside and tried doing the daily tasks he would encounter as an amputee. Later, through the course of many hours of telephone conversations with me, he became convinced that living with a hand amputation wouldn't be a problem. Fortunately I had something like 30 years of experience to relate to him and I could be very truthful in answering his questions. In our conversations I was always very careful not to be persuasive, but to try to be truthful and factual in how I got along with one hand so he could come to his own conclusions.

Eventually Frank "did it." he became an amputee through a staged accident. Fortunately I'm able to report that his loss has been very successful and he is now a very happy amputee. He had far less pain than I encountered and much less than even he expected. He had little difficulty adapting to using one hand while his stump healed. He was very pleased when he got his prosthesis and related that he wished he had done it when he was in his 20s and had not waited so long. Because he had a very positive outlook, his friends took his "accident" in stride and he went on with his life as if nothing ever happened. This is a case of a very successful elective self-amputation, in part due to much careful planning and research.

"Carlos" came to America from south of the border in his teens. When he was about six years of age, he too saw a one-handed man who wore a hook. He and his father were walking down a street when a well-dress hombre stepped out of a car and confidently strolled across the street and into a building in front of them. Carlos only saw his hook for only a few seconds, but he remembered it for ever.

After he graduated from high school, he worked at a machine shop where he staged an "accident" to cut off his hand. The event took off his intended hand, but also accidently amputated most of his "good" hand too. He was left without a thumb and only two useful fingers on his remaining hand. His recovery was long and painful. Intentional amputation accidents can be risky.

Life with one hook and two only somewhat useful fingers was very difficult for Carlos, and the pain in his remaining partial hand continued. To make life easier for him, I suggested he try a special rubber-tipped typing hook on his prosthesis such as the one which I made out of a piece of aluminum tubing. He had one made by a friend and found it very helpful. He could now type with one finger and one hook. It was much faster than typing with one finger alone!

Fortunately his wife was very understanding, she was a very rare individual. He had told her about his elective amputation when they first met and she had no problem with this unusual desire. She was able to help him get along with of his partial hand problem. To improve his life they considered every possible alternative, including amputation of his partial hand and continuing life with two hooks.

They decided to try to save and improve the functionality of his partial hand and he underwent reconstructive surgery where one of his toes was transplanted to replace his missing thumb. It was successful and at last he had a more functional hand and could continue his life as a returning college student.

The above stories illustrate the lengths to which AID inflicted people will go to become amputees. Self-amputation is indeed a risky business. They highlight the need for further research and understanding of this condition. It is not known if this syndrome is hereditary or learned. As we have heard, many recall seeing amputees at an early age which may trigger the development of an AID.

Therapy alone does not seem to cure this syndrome, but it can help some deal with the amputation desire. The medical profession has not yet reached the point where it will willingly preform elective amputations in America. Physicians first basic principle is "to do your patient no harm." They see amputation as debilitating. Hospitals will not allow these procedures because of fear of adverse public reaction. It is clear that the AID condition merits further investigation and understanding.

Those who have accomplished a successful amputation express their satisfaction with their new condition and seem to go on to a fulfilled and happy new life style. From my personal experience of over 30 years, I can say in all truthfulness that I have never had any regrets. My life has been happy and successful. Having only one hand has not prevented me leading an active and outdoor lifestyle. The few tasks that I am unable to do, such as playing a piano, are not important to me. At the same time, I have never had any desire for any further amputations. I am very content with my present one-handed condition.

Hopefully this writing will ease the anxiety and trepidation of those who are afflicted with the Amputee Identity Disorder condition at a time when there is very little out there on the subject. It is unfortunate that those who are afflicted must undergo the trauma and anxiety of performing their own haphazard amputations because society has not evolved to the extent which will allow safe and painless surgical limb removal where it is deemed appropriate. In time, further research will undoubtedly lead to a better understanding and acceptance of this condition and perhaps even it's elimination all together.

To my knowledge, as of this date, I am the first person to ever go public about the AID condition. In doing so I hope my efforts will ease the frustration and guilt feelings of those afflicted and be somewhat of a comfort to them. I welcome any questions, or feedback on this subject. Feel free to contact me at ed@quietworld.org.

Printed in the United States
by Baker & Taylor Publisher Services

Printed in the United States
by Baker & Taylor Publisher Services